Marketing Models

Kim Buch-Madsen (ed.), Ole E. Andersen,
Birgitte W. Grandjean, Christian Grandjean, Heidi Hansen,
Niels Kühl Hasager, Svend Hollensen, Sine Nørholm Just,
Jan Kyhnau, David Juul Ledstrup, Michael Sjørvad & Kim Skjoldborg

Marketing Models

Samfundslitteratur

Kim Buch-Madsen (ed.), Ole E. Andersen, Birgitte W. Grandjean, Christian Grandjean, Heidi Hansen, Niels Kühl Hasager, Svend Hollensen, Sine Nørholm Just, Jan Kyhnau, David Juul Ledstrup, Michael Sjørvad & Kim Skjoldborg

Marketing Models

1st edition 2019

© The authors and Samfundslitteratur 2019

Editor: Henrik Schjerning
Copy editor: Kevin Ploug Knudsen
Cover: Imperiet (Jes Madsen)
Typeset: Ane Svendsen, SL grafik (slgrafik.dk)
Icons: Boston/BCG model, Value Proposition Canvas, Business Model Canvas: Designed by Freepik for Flaticon.com. Social Media Landscape: Designed by Madebyoliver for Flaticon.com.
Fonts: Franklin Gothic and Minion Pro
Print: Latgales Druka

ISBN: 978-87-593-3201-6

Samfundslitteratur
info@samfundslitteratur.dk
samfundslitteratur.dk

All rights reserved

Copies may only be made by institutions or companies that have entered into an agreement with Copydan Text & Node, and only within the limits specified in the agreement. The only exception is short extracts used for reviews.

CONTENTS

INTRODUCTION   9

1. MACRO ENVIRONMENT, MARKET AND CUSTOMERS

PESTEL   14
By Christian Grandjean

SMP (SEGMENTATION PROCESS)   18
By Kim Buch-Madsen

PERCEIVED RISK   22
By Niels Kühl Hasager

BUYING MOTIVES ON B2C MARKETS   26
By Ole E. Andersen

SOCIAL BUYING MOTIVES   30
By Niels Kühl Hasager

KANO'S CUSTOMER SATISFACTION MODEL   34
By Birgitte W. Grandjean

THE BUYING PROCESS ON B2B MARKETS (BUY GRID)   38
By Kim Buch-Madsen

FCB-MODEL   42
By Ole E. Andersen

NET PROMOTER SCORE   46
By Ole E. Andersen

MARKETING RESEARCH PROCESS   50
By Ole E. Andersen

2. MARKETING MIX AND VALUE PACK

8 P (MARKETING MIX)   56
By Ole E. Andersen

THE FIVE PRODUCT DIMENSIONS   60
By Birgitte W. Grandjean

SERVICE TRIANGLE   64
By Kim Buch-Madsen

CUSTOMER VALUE   68
By Kim Buch-Madsen

VALUE PROPOSITION CANVAS   74
By Jan Kyhnau

AAKER'S BRAND IDENTITY PLANNING MODEL   80
By Heidi Hansen

THE CUSTOMER-BASED BRAND EQUITY MODEL (CBBE)   84
By Heidi Hansen

BRAND ARCHITECTURE   88
By Heidi Hansen

DISTRIBUTION STRATEGY (PLACE)   94
By Kim Buch-Madsen

3. MARKET COMMUNICATION AND SALES

TIBBLE'S PLANNING CYCLE   102
By Sine Nørholm Just

THE COMMUNICATION PROCESS   106
By Kim Skjoldborg

PAID, OWNED AND EARNED MEDIA MODEL   112
By Christian Grandjean

AIDA   116
By Ole E. Andersen

DAGMAR   120
By Sine Nørholm Just

EFFECTIVE FREQUENCY (IN MEDIA PLANNING)   124
By Ole E. Andersen

THE SALES PROCESS   128
By Kim Buch-Madsen

SALES MANAGEMENT   132
By Michael Sjørvad

4. STRATEGY AND INNOVATION

BOSTON/BCG MODEL   140
By Kim Buch-Madsen

ANSOFF'S MATRIX   144
By Kim Buch-Madsen

PORTER'S FIVE FORCES   148
By Kim Buch-Madsen

PORTER'S GENERIC COMPETITIVE STRATEGIES   154
By Christian Grandjean

BLUE OCEAN STRATEGY   160
By Christian Grandjean

BUSINESS MODEL CANVAS   166
By Kim Buch-Madsen

ROGERS' ADOPTION CURVE   172
By Kim Buch-Madsen

PRODUCT LIFE CYCLE (PLC)   178
By Kim Buch-Madsen

STAGE-GATE MODEL   182
By Kim Buch-Madsen

5. GLOBAL MARKETING AND ONLINE MARKETING

FIVE PHASES OF INTERNATIONALIZATION   188
By Svend Hollensen

INTERNATIONAL COMPETITIVENESS – FROM MACRO TO MICRO   192
By Svend Hollensen

HOLLENSEN'S MARKET ASSESSMENT MODEL   196
By Svend Hollensen

FUNNEL MODEL FOR INTERNATIONAL MARKET SELECTION (IMS)   200
By Svend Hollensen

HOLLENSEN'S MODEL FOR "ENTRY MODE" CHOICE   204
By Svend Hollensen

HOLLENSEN'S GLOCALIZATION MODEL   208
By Svend Hollensen

DIGITAL MARKETING MIX   212
By Kim Skjoldborg

SOCIAL MEDIA LANDSCAPE   216
By David Juul Ledstrup

COMPREHENSIVE SOCIAL MEDIA STRATEGY   220
By David Juul Ledstrup

AUTHOR PROFILES   223

INTRODUCTION

The purpose of this book is to provide something that we think the market is missing: an overview of the marketing field's most important models and a handbook on how to use them, assembled in one place, in one small handy book.

Models are tools to describe, understand, and incite action. Some models are best used for describing and understanding marketing practices and theories, others best for prompting action, and yet others meet both. All models are a generalized simplification of reality, and therefore they must always be "translated" to the specific marketing situation you may find yourself in. They are created for a general situation and not for your specific situation. No model includes all relevant aspects; models are characterized by capturing something and omitting something else.

Finally, no one model is always 100 % valid. A good model illustrates how components usually are related and suggest possible courses of action.

We let these facts and the situation in which you're using the model shape the structure of the book. Therefore, all the models of the book follow the same template and answer the same three questions:

- What is the model about?
- How can you use the model?
- What are the shortcomings and weaknesses of the model?

Marketing Models has the ability to stand alone for business use, but in academic situations, it works best in combination with a good basic marketing textbook.

Marketing is a large field that contains many great models, and it has been an exciting challenge to choose from these models. We have selected the book's models according to the following criteria: validity, relevancy, pedagogy, and user-friendliness, and the book contains the models we regard as the most important.

We may expand the book in a later edition, so we would love to hear from you if there are any models you feel are missing.

It has been an exciting learning process to write this book. We hope you find it equally exciting and enlightening to read. Above all, we hope that it will be a useful partner in your marketing studies or marketing job.

We wish you all the best in your work and have fun with *Marketing Models!*

1. MACRO ENVIRONMENT, MARKET AND CUSTOMERS

PESTEL
By Christian Grandjean

PESTEL
Political factors (Politics)
Economic and Demographic factors (Economy)
Social and Cultural factors (Social)
Technological factors (Technology)
Environmental factors (Environment)
Legal factors (Legal)

INTRODUCTION

The PESTEL model is used to analyze the macro-environmental factors that can impact a business. The purpose is to detect threats and opportunities as early as possible.

WHAT IS THE MODEL ABOUT?

PESTEL is a simple and straightforward model that assists a company to understand the external factors that affect its business affairs, for example, laws, special cultural traditions or new technology.

The model can be used as a supplement to the Porter Five Forces model. The information from the PESTEL model can typically be used in a SWOT model.

The PESTEL model is a modern variant of the PEST model from the mid-1960s. You may come across the model in other variants (e.g., STEP, PESTE-LONG). They are all built on the same foundation but cover different factors.

The model lists six overall parameters. A number of questions relevant to the situation to be analyzed must be formulated for each parameter. If a company considers introducing a new, healthy drink in a market, a certain set of questions must be asked, whereas, in other another context, it is relevant to pose a different set of questions. For a healthy drink, the questions may be:

- **Political affairs:** Is there any political interest in or resistance to healthy drinks? Are there any regional (i.e., European Union) rules or national laws related to these products? Are there any special considerations in terms of trade organizations and interest groups?
- **Economy and demography:** What is the overall economic situation? Is there growth or slowdown? Is there purchasing power for new, health-oriented products? How is the population divided by age, sex, and religion? What is the number of households, and how are they divided into singles, married couples or other family forms? Who is spending money on healthy products, and when?
- **Social and cultural conditions:** What are social conditions of the market? Are there public health services? Are there local conditions (national, regional and local) of which to be aware? What's trendy, for example, the health-ori-

ented or the political consumer? When and how does the target group use and consume healthy products?
- **Technological conditions:** What influence does technological development have on the market? Would it be relevant to market the new drink through digital channels? Who uses which channels when? Do production and food technology increase the attractiveness of the health product?
- **Environmental conditions:** Are there any special environmental conditions to be aware of? Is there a focus on raw materials and origin? Is there attention on energy consumption associated with the production? Should the packaging be recycled?
- **Legislation:** Are there any new laws, rules, and regulations being developed? Are there any rules for product declarations and marketing of health products?

HOW CAN YOU USE THE MODEL?

The PESTEL model describes macro-environmental factors for a specific business, product or marketing situation, but is not intended for general macro environment analysis.

Therefore, it is most useful for a company facing significant actions or changes. For example, the model can be used to draw a picture of the company's outside world and identify important areas of which be aware, if for example, considering whether or not to enter a new market or launch a new product.

The model reveals opportunities and threats. The more threats, the more difficult it is, requiring increased planning for upcoming efforts.

WHAT ARE THE SHORTCOMINGS AND WEAKNESSES OF THE MODEL?

When working with the PESTEL model, it is easy to be led to describe the past or to draw too general of a picture of a current situation. Therefore, it is important to continuously ensure the identified threats and opportunities are relevant to the business and task beforehand. For example, it is important to be aware of the threats and opportunities related to the planned marketing of a given product, if that is the task you are facing.

You should also consider whether you are performing an analysis of the overall circumstances in the immediate present, or if you are taking into account future opportunities and threats, as well.

It is equally valuable to be aware of the different parameters that can affect the business both now and in the long run. A new law or technology can, from day to day, create new business opportunities or seriously affect existing businesses. Social and cultural development typically takes place over a long period of time though.

Finally, it is worth noting the six parameters of the model do not work as isolated sections as the model gives the impression of. Therefore, it can be difficult to know where in the model threats and opportunities should be placed. Environmental factors (e.g., a political requirement for package recycling) can also be classified as a political factor (that is a law). It is, therefore, a good idea to list threats and opportunities where they are considered most relevant to the company.

REFERENCES

Andersen, Ole E., Svend Hollensen, Poul K. Faarup et al. (2016). *Moderne markedsføring*, 2nd edition. Copenhagen: Hans Reitzels Forlag.

Thomas, Howard (2007). An Analysis of the Environment and Competitive Dynamics of Management Education. *Journal of Management Development*, 26 (1): 9-21.

Yüksel, Ihsan (2012). Developing a Multi-Criteria Decision Making Model for PESTEL Analysis. *International Journal of Business and Management*, 7 (24): 52-66.

SMP (SEGMENTATION PROCESS)

By Kim Buch-Madsen

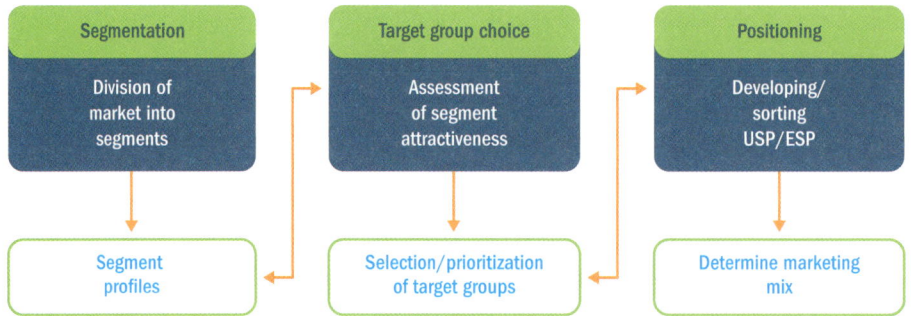

INTRODUCTION

The model demonstrates a systematic approach to segmenting the market and selecting target group(s). The purpose is to distinguish target groups that are attractive in terms of sales potential, competition, company goals and resources, as well as having common behavioral characteristics. This allows marketing efforts to be targeted accurately, and thus, more likely be effective.

WHAT IS THE MODEL ABOUT?

The model is a working method divided into stages, gradually progressing to the most attractive target group(s) and determining strategy and marketing mix for each target group.

Ideally, the process must lead to target groups that are measurable, profitable, accessible, mutually differentiated, and realistic in terms of competitive conditions and company resources.

In the first stage, *"Segment profiles"*, the market is divided into segments according to criteria relevant to the market and the company. In B2C markets, the most common criteria are geographical, demographic, psychological, and behavioral. In B2B markets, industry, size, location, production conditions, purchasing organization and demand factors, such as delivery time, order size or price level are often used. This creates profiles (short descriptions) of market segments.

In the next stage, *"Selection/prioritization of target groups"*, the segments' attractiveness are evaluated with the same standards as when considering market attractiveness. There will often be a focus on conditions such as volume, growth, purchasing power, price sensitivity, competitive conditions, bargaining power, and competitive intensity. Hereafter, the most attractive target groups for the company are selected and prioritized. It is important to carefully assess which target groups are most attractive to the company. A target group is not necessarily attractive because it is large or because the competitors seek it. It is a common error to select the largest target groups or target groups similar to competitors because it is possible to face such fierce competition that it is not profitable. Therefore, it is a well-known competitive strategy to divide the market differently than the competitors and/or identify target groups overlooked or under-prioritized by the competition.

The final stage, *"Determine marketing mix"*, is about how to adapt the positioning and marketing mix for the individual target group and to what extent. A nondifferentiated strategy utilizes an identical marketing mix for all target groups and is cost-effective but not as accurate. A differentiated strategy customizes the marketing mix to each target group and is more precise, but it also results in higher costs. In a focused strategy, the company chooses only one target group and puts all its effort behind it. The advantages are specialization and limited costs, but on the other hand, the market potential is limited to only one target group. This final stage provides the foundation for concrete marketing planning and lays out how and to what extent the 8 Ps in the marketing mix (see 8 P model, page 56) should be tailored to each target group.

HOW CAN YOU USE THE MODEL?

The model demonstrates a practical working procedure for segmentation and target group selection, and also shows what considerations and choices should be made and in which order. You may come across variations of the model in different textbooks, but the logic of the workflow is the same.

A segmentation can easily become extensive and unnecessarily complicated, so "keeping it simple" is a good rule of thumb for many companies. For example, one to three segmentation criteria is usually enough. More criteria can quickly complicate and hinder the process.

WHAT ARE THE SHORTCOMINGS AND WEAKNESSES OF THE MODEL?

The model is an ideal type model, meaning it demonstrates a workflow that usually – but not always – will apply. In addition, it is a fairly general model that shows which decisions and tasks are to be performed but not how. For example, the model does not provide guidelines for how to divide the market into segments, how to assess the attractiveness of each segment, or how to customize the marketing mix for the chosen target groups.

The model is also available in several variations, some with more stages, some with less. However, the order and logic of each stage are roughly the same, although different authors choose different degrees of detail.

Finally, it can be argued that the model should include a final stage in which the company evaluates the results of the marketing and assesses whether the right target groups have been selected or whether changes should be made.

REFERENCES

Andersen, Finn Rolighed, Bjarne Warming Jensen, Mette Risgaard Olsen et al. (2015). *International markedsføring*, 5th edition. Copenhagen: Trojka.

Andersen, Ole E., Svend Hollensen, Poul K. Faarup et al. (2016). *Moderne markedsføring*, 2nd edition. Copenhagen: Hans Reitzels Forlag.

Buch-Madsen, Kim (2005). *Marketing – klart og koncentreret*. Frederiksberg: Samfundslitteratur.

Dietrich, Timo, Sharyn Rundle-Thiele & Krzysztof Kubacki (2017). *Segmentation in Social Marketing – Process, Methods and Application*. Singapore: Springer.

Jobber, David & Fiona Ellis-Chadwick (2016). *Principles and Practice of Marketing*, 8th edition. Maidenhead: McGraw-Hill Education.

McDonald, Malcolm & Ian Dunbar (2015). *Market Segmentation – How to Do It and How to Profit from It*, 4th edition. Chichester: John Wiley & Sons.

PERCEIVED RISK
By Niels Kühl Hasager

TYPE OF PERCEIVED RISK	EXAMPLES
Financial risk	• Am I making a financially sound purchase? • Is there a better alternative at the same price? • Will there be follow-up costs, such as repairs?
Physical risk	• Is the product dangerous to my family or me? • Is the product safely secured, for example, a protective cover for a lawnmower?
Functional risk	• Will the product give me maximum value? • Does the outerwear provide the promised water repellency?
Social risk	• Will I be teased or ridiculed by my colleagues if I acquire this item? • Will my family approve of my purchase of, e.g., a new bike?
Psychological risk	• Will my or my family's needs actually be met by this purchase? • Will I still like the painting in three weeks? • Will I feel stupid if I cannot figure out the app?
Time risk	• Am I spending too much time to obtain the product? Does the online payment take too long to process? • Am I spending too much time locating the product or manufacturer?

INTRODUCTION

The model demonstrates six different types of perceived risk that a consumer or group may experience when considering purchasing a product or service. Perceived risk is a negative association and can prevent a purchase. As a result, the company must seek to minimize this effect through effective marketing.

WHAT IS THE MODEL ABOUT?

When a consumer purchases a product or service, they experience possible undesirable consequences of the purchase. The model deals with the consumer's subjective perceived risk.

Research indicates that people psychologically do not like risks, and therefore, the consumer will act in different ways to avoid or reduce this perceived risk. For example, they may seek additional information from the manufacturer, in stores, compare options and seek alternatives, get advice from family, friends or social media, and read reviews on websites like TripAdvisor, Trustpilot, etc.

The model structures this barrier for purchases in six different types of perceived risk that have been shown among consumers. As a result, the company gets six concrete fixed points to guide its efforts in helping the consumer avoid or minimize risk, thereby increasing the chance of sales.

HOW CAN YOU USE THE MODEL?

Overall, the model can flesh out perceived risks, thereby providing an understanding of the uncertainties consumers experience.

In addition, the model can be used as a basis for describing or analyzing the purchasing behavior of a given target group, for example, suggesting interesting topics to be investigated in market research. In diagnostic situations, the model is helpful, for example, in explaining why sales do not rise as anticipated, despite well-planned marketing. Is the target experiencing risks that have not been taken into account and preventing sales?

The model is best utilized when compiling a list of factors that can hamper or prevent the customer from purchasing. The six types of risk help the company to target its efforts in removing or minimizing consumers' perceived risks through marketing, thereby increasing the likelihood the customer makes a purchase. Common methods include:

- Transparency in market offers, making it easy to evaluate and compare products
- Credible references in market communications (testimonials)
- Strong brand, often limiting or even eliminating the experienced risk
- Warranty and exchange options
- Opportunity to try or taste an item before purchasing
- Hotline and support.

WHAT ARE THE SHORTCOMINGS AND WEAKNESSES OF THE MODEL?

Many textbook reproductions have modified the model to include a time-related risk, reflecting the businesses of today's society. Technological and consumer development may indicate that the model, in the future, must be expanded to include new dimensions of perceived risk.

These six types of risk are not mutually exclusive. Most often, several risk factors will apply to the same consumer or target group. Different risks can overlap and interact with each other; they should be evaluated in conjunction with one another. Loss of status, for example, is a psychological factor that occurs in social interaction. Certain experienced physical risks may be psychologically contingent, e.g., dental visits or flights. Functional risks may become physical, such as an unstable smoke alarm or a defective car brake.

REFERENCES

Andersen, Finn Rolighed, Bjarne Warming Jensen, Mette Risgaard Olsen et al. (2015). *International markedsføring*, 5th edition. Copenhagen: Trojka.

Andersen, Ole E., Svend Hollensen, Poul K. Faarup et al. (2016). *Moderne markedsføring*, 2nd edition. Copenhagen: Hans Reitzels Forlag.

Kotler, Philip T. & Kevin Lane Keller (2012). *Marketing Management*, 14th edition. Harlow: Pearson Education Limited.

Tian-Que, Liu (2012). "Perceived Risk in Marketing Strategy". In Min Zhu (ed.), *Business, Economics, Financial Sciences, and Management*. Heidelberg: Springer: 175-178.

BUYING MOTIVES ON B2C MARKETS
By Ole E. Andersen

NEGATIVE MOTIVES	EXAMPLES	POSITIVE MOTIVES	EXAMPLES
Problem removal	Pain relievers, vacuum cleaner, mouse trap	Sensory gratification	Great movie, eating out, vacations, delicious perfume
Problem prevention	Insurance, car service, motion sickness pills	Cognitive stimulation/performance	Good book, reading the newspaper, computer games, lectures
Conflict positive-negative	Low-calorie beer	Social approval	Fancy clothes, good looks, new car, good at eSports
Reduced satisfaction	Bad fitness center, I switch to another		
Empty shelves	We need to buy coffee because we are out of coffee		

INTRODUCTION

The model is a simple but very useful breakdown of consumer motivations for buying products or services in basic negative and positive motives, and it is a great tool for discussing possible positioning strategies.

WHAT IS THE MODEL ABOUT?

The model classifies all products or services based on which motives or "drivers" the consumers primarily have, or are assumed to have to buy and consume. The negative motives can be summarized as products that are *problem solvers*, while positively motivated purchases are driven by consumers' intentions of realizing desires and *dreams*. The model can be used at any product category level, but with an even greater reward at the brand level, if the various brands in a category are positioned differently, or desire to be positioned differently.

The model covers every purchase situation, including the fundamentally negative motivated shift of behavior as a result of dissatisfaction and routine purchases without a motive other than to simply fill the shelves of the household and stock up.

In the aforementioned scenario, the primary motive is not a direct result of current marketing activities. It constitutes a repeat purchase of the same brand, reflecting the customer's built-up brand loyalty, which possibly can be reactivated with a reminder advertisement close to the place or time of purchase.

HOW CAN YOU USE THE MODEL?

First and foremost, the model provides a platform to reflect on what motives serve as the basis for the purchase or use of a product or service. The model applies to *all* purchases as opposed to the Social Buying Motives model (page 30), which is relevant only if a purchase, use, or possession of a product is *partly* dependent on what other people think.

The usability of the model for motive-based positioning can be stressed by some additional features of the two types of buying motives. The concept of *negative motives* is based on the intuitive insight that the consumer will make the purchase with a sense of *relief*, that being problem removal, prevention, etc. It is *necessary* purchases that do not bring much pleasure ("need to have/to do"). To make the purchase decision, information and possibly demonstrations of what the product can do to reduce the negative state is needed. The positioning of the products must, therefore, take place with an emphasis on their *functional features* and *benefits*, which can facilitate consumers' everyday life, serving as the primary motive for product use. The differentiation between brands in the product category shall hereinafter be based on the specific characteristics and advantages offered by the product.

With the three *positive buying motives,* the case is completely opposite. Purchase, possession, and use are *rewarding* and changing in that they lead the customer to a new, heightened state of satisfaction ("nice to have/do"). The products are bought and used with joy and pleasure. For those decisions, it is more seduction than facts that can lead to attention and interest in the product. The positioning should, therefore, be based on *emotional motives* and show *positive effects* of product use. Within these overall positioning dimensions, each brand must find its unique character.

WHAT ARE THE SHORTCOMINGS AND WEAKNESSES OF THE MODEL?

The main problem with the model is that the nature of certain products makes it difficult to accurately identify consumer motives as either positive or negative because, in reality, our motives can be two-sided or complex. For example, think of toothpaste, which can be problem removal (bad breath), problem prevention (against cavities), enjoyment and pleasure (nice, fresh taste), and receiving social approval (white teeth). It is then an additional task to identify the primary and secondary motives for a given target group.

Another weakness is that product categories with a wide range of prices and brand images and, thus, very different target groups can use the model only on a brand level. Think of cars that cannot be uniquely identified with one specific purchase motive. Purchasing a cheap car, like a KIA Picanto, may be motivated by problem prevention (longer commute to work) while buying a Golf Convertible for most buyers is likely to have a prominent element of positive buying motives (enjoyment and social approval). A third deficiency of the model is that buying motives for a product category are general and do not provide indications of which *specific* product characteristics and/or types of desirable effects would be motivating. It requires primary data collection and consumer analysis. This is particularly true for smaller brands or new brands. It may be more important for them to find a niche based on insights from small audiences and position themselves on different dimensions compared to larger brands.

REFERENCES

Andersen, Ole E. (2014). *Forstå forbrugerne og bliv en bedre markedsfører*. Frederiksberg: Samfundslitteratur.

Andersen, Ole E., Svend Hollensen, Poul K. Faarup et al. (2016). *Moderne markedsføring*, 2nd edition. Copenhagen: Hans Reitzels Forlag.

Rossiter, John & Larry Percy (1997). *Advertising Communications and Promotion Management*, 2nd edition. New York: McGraw-Hill.

Solomon, Michael R., Gary J. Bamossy, Søren T. Askegaard et al. (2016). *Consumer Behaviour. A European Perspective,* 6th edition. Harlow: Pearson Education Limited.

SOCIAL BUYING MOTIVES
By Niels Kühl Hasager

SOCIAL BUYING MOTIVE	FEATURES	EXAMPLE
Snob (different)	The snob purchase motive is activated when a product or service is purchased to portray that you are unique.	When a person buys a special hand-knitted sweater or specially imported coffee from Columbia.
Veblen (expensive)	The Veblen purchase motive is activated when a product or service is purchased to show that you can afford it and are financially resourceful.	When a person purchases luxury brands like Cartier, expensive wines, or goes to an expensive hairdresser.
Bandwagon (alike)	The bandwagon purchase motive is activated when a product or service is purchased to show you buy and behave like everyone else.	When a person buys items, their friends have already bought, for example, Levi's cowboy jeans or Netflix.
Thrifty (inexpensive)	A thrifty purchase motive is activated when a product or service is purchased to show you are frugal by buying cheaply and efficiently.	When a person buys goods on sale or shops at stores with generally low prices, e.g., Netto.

INTRODUCTION

The model demonstrates four relevant buying motives when consumers allow their choice of products and brands to be influenced by what other people think and do. It may be an attempt to adapt to others, or on the contrary, an attempt to stand out from the crowd.

WHAT IS THE MODEL ABOUT?

There is a distinction between functional, personal, situational, and social buying motives. This model demonstrates four possible influential social purchasing motives and the driving force each motive relies upon.

It also demonstrates how social buying motives can be about copying others to try to fit in, as well as the different ways to stand out and be unique. Studies have shown that we are not as guided by functional or rational motives as we think or want to be, but are more often guided by social motives.

HOW CAN YOU USE THE MODEL?

The model is primarily for B2C markets. Although social motives can also play a certain role in B2B purchases, they rarely play a decisive role.

Overall, the model details an understanding of how our consumption patterns can be strongly influenced by what other people do, think, and believe. At the same time, the model provides four easily understood and useful types of social buying motives.

The model can be used to identify which social drivers influence or control consumer purchases, and thereby what motivations to tap into in marketing and communication efforts. Awareness of a target group's possible social buying motives is helpful in creating messaging and choosing formats and media, and increase the likelihood of achieving the goal and triggering sales.

For analysis purposes, for example, the model can be used to formulate hypotheses regarding consumers' expected behavior prior to conducting the analysis. It can also be used to discover socially-contemplated motive patterns in unstructured customer data.

WHAT ARE THE SHORTCOMINGS AND WEAKNESSES OF THE MODEL?

Social buying motives do not apply to all consumer purchases but are valid in some cases.

Buying motives are rarely either-or but usually a combination of several types of motives within the functional, personal, situational and social buying motives. Thus, the model appears to be a bit narrow as it only includes social buying motives. Buying motives will often be related to consumer demographics, such as age, income and/or psychographic characteristics, such as lifestyle. The model does not take this into account.

At the macro level, the model does not include how economic and political contexts can affect consumers' buying motives. During the financial crisis, from 2008 onward, there were clear evidence consumers became more cautious and price-conscious, and that thrifty motives became more dominant.

REFERENCES

Andersen, Finn Rolighed, Bjarne Warming Jensen, Mette Risgaard Olsen et al. (2015). *International markedsføring*, 5th edition. Copenhagen: Trojka.

Andersen, Ole E., Svend Hollensen, Poul K. Faarup et al. (2016). *Moderne markedsføring*, 2nd edition. Copenhagen: Hans Reitzels Forlag.

Donovan, Rob & Nadine Henley (2010). *Principles and Practice of Social Marketing – An International Perspective*. Cambridge: Cambridge University Press.

Jansson-Boyd, Cathrine V. & Magdalena J. Zawisza (2017). *Routledge International Handbook of Consumer Psychology*. New York: Routledge.

KANO'S CUSTOMER SATISFACTION MODEL
By Birgitte W. Grandjean

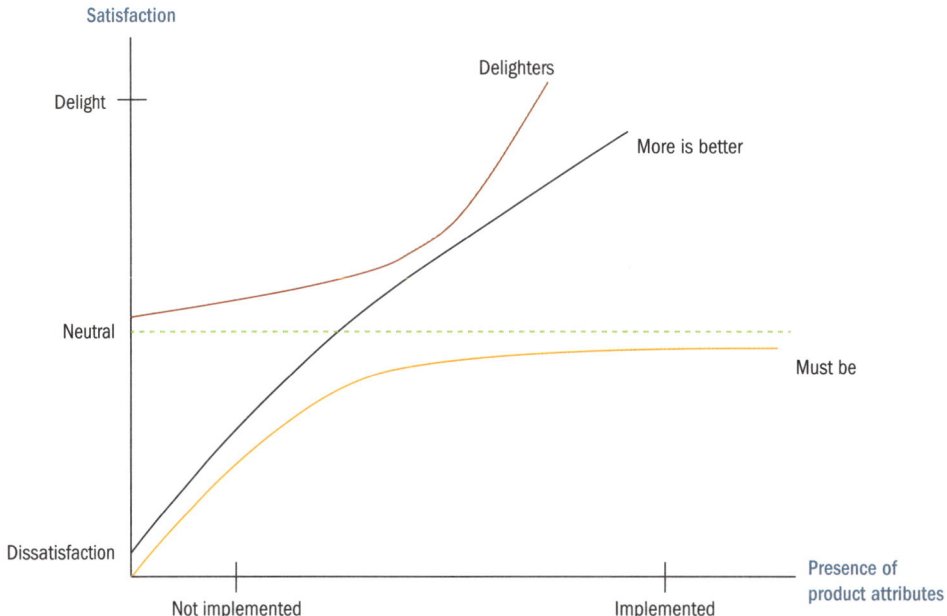

INTRODUCTION

Kano's model describes three different types of product attributes, which each create a dimension of customer satisfaction. The model also shows that satisfaction and dissatisfaction are different beyond just high and low satisfaction, and therefore they each have their own curves.

WHAT IS THE MODEL ABOUT?

In markets with fierce competition where customers quickly share good or bad experiences online, it is important the company does more than seek to make the customer happy. It is equally important to ensure that the customer is not dissatisfied and that the customer is not just satisfied, but also both happy and excited.

Kano's model can help identify 1) what ensures that the customer is not dissatisfied, 2) what it takes for the customer to perceive the product attractively, and 3) what will surprise the customer and create enthusiasm.

Kano divides product attributes into three categories:

- Must be
- More is better
- Delighters.

Must be: These are the basic product attributes that customers take for granted, which allows the product to compete in the market. In other words, it is the characteristics customers only discover if they are missing, and therefore the product does not meet customers' basic requirements when purchasing the product.

An example of a *Must be* could be that in a restaurant you have a table at which to sit, a menu from which to choose, and food that meets the expected quality.

More is better: However, it is not enough to meet the customer's basic expectations. This can, at most, prevent customer dissatisfaction. It is usually important to offer something to exceed the expectation. According to the model, it is referred to as *More is better* and include product attributes that increase customer satisfaction because he or she receives something more than expected. It is on these characteristics that most products compete; they differentiate products from each other and influence the customer's willingness to purchase a product.

An example of *More is better* could be a restaurant that is decorated in a special way, plays atmospheric music, and has a high level of service.

Delighters: There is a limit as to how many product characteristics a customer finds relevant and have an interest in. In order to maintain customer interest and satisfaction, there is often a need for something extra to raise enthusiasm.

A *Delighter* offers the customer a positive surprise, something they did not know they needed but they would be happy with. Some wow effect. Although only a few Delighters are affiliated with a product, it can significantly increase customer satisfaction.

On the other hand, it will not cause dissatisfaction if the Delighter is left out, as it is not expected. An example of Delighters at a restaurant could be an opportunity to retrieve recipes or descriptions of the ingredients on the restaurant's website.

The primary competition is on the *More is better* qualities. On the other hand, *Must be* and *Delighters*, respectively, are the negative and positive surprises that can create extraordinary problems or opportunities, and are, therefore, crucial to consider. Finally, it is important to keep in mind that you cannot create customer satisfaction without *Must be-product* characteristics that fully meet customer expectations. Not even multiple well-composed *More is better* or *Delighters* will create excitement if the foundation is not solid.

HOW CAN YOU USE THE MODEL?

The model can be used as a starting point to identify the *Must be* minimum requirements that may result in lost customers or create shitstorms if they are neglected. Similarly, the model can be used to provide customers *Delighters*, which can really differentiate the company's products from other providers, creating ambassadors and positive word-of-mouth recommendations.

Finally, the model's three satisfaction attributes can be used to distinguish between the middle *More is better* curve, where the majority of competition takes place, and the *Must be* and *Delighters* extremes, which implies the extraordinary risks and opportunities.

WHAT ARE THE SHORTCOMINGS AND WEAKNESSES OF THE MODEL?

The model does not take into account there may be different customer groups for the same product and that customers can be influenced by very different lifestyles. One customer group at an Italian restaurant may think it is absolutely perfect with a family-friendly atmosphere and a child-friendly menu. Conversely, another customer group might appreciate an authentic Italian "La Familia atmosphere," but at the same time want something different than pizza and lasagna.

Another challenge for the model is that today's customers are characterized by an individualistic and situational buying behavior. This makes it more difficult to collect the necessary, credible customer insights that Kano's model requires.

Situational and individualistic consumer behavior also makes it more difficult to categorize and standardize solutions. What satisfies a person in one situation does not mean that it also works in another situation.

Finally, the model does not capture the dynamics of the markets. Businesses constantly add new things to compete, and competitors quickly imitate what works. Therefore, the *More is better* attributes that worked yesterday may be *Must be* attributes tomorrow. Similarly, *Delighters* can quickly lose their wow effect if they are imitated.

REFERENCES

Andersen, Finn Rolighed, Bjarne Warming Jensen, Mette Risgaard Olsen et al. (2015). *International markedsføring*, 5th edition. Copenhagen: Trojka.

Andersen, Ole E., Svend Hollensen, Poul K. Faarup et al. (2016). *Moderne markedsføring*, 2nd edition. Copenhagen: Hans Reitzels Forlag.

Cohen, Lou (1995). *Quality Function Deployment: How to Make QFD Work for You*. Reading: Addison-Wesley.

Jobber, David (2007). "Fundamentals of Modern Marketing Thought." I David Jobber (ed.), *Principles and Practice of Marketing*. London: McGraw-Hill Education. https://www.mheducation.co.uk/he/chapters/9780077140007.pdf (retrieved 01.03.17).

THE BUYING PROCESS ON B2B MARKETS (BUY GRID)

By Kim Buch-Madsen

PURCHASE PROCESS	NEW PURCHASE	MODIFIED REPURCHASE	ROUTINE PURCHASE
Recognition of Problem	Yes	Maybe	No
Description Needs	Yes	Maybe	No
Specification Requirements	Yes	Yes	Yes
Supplier Search	Yes	Maybe	No
Qualifying Subjects	Yes	Maybe	No
Supplier Selection	Yes	Maybe	No
Delivery, Payment, etc.	Yes	Yes	Yes
Continuing Follow-up	Yes	Yes	Yes

INTRODUCTION

The model describes the order of phases a company typically goes through in the buying process and how the degree of novelty influences each phase.

WHAT IS THE MODEL ABOUT?

The model describes phases that the customer goes through during a purchase; from need recognition to purchase, evaluation and follow-up. Whether the customer goes through all phases or just some of them depends on what type of purchase it is. The model distinguishes between new purchases, routine purchases, and modified repurchases.

For *new purchases*, the customer has no or limited experience and/or it is a complex or costly purchase. For *routine purchases*, the customer repurchases a known product from a supplier they already know. The *modified repurchase* is in the middle where the customer purchases a known product, but in a modified version or with other suppliers.

The logic behind the model is that the more novel the purchase is, the greater the risk and the uncertainty. Therefore, the customer experiences greater informational needs and the buying process becomes more thorough, meaning more phases.

The individual phases can be illustrated by the following example: a company that markets herbal medicines launches a new product, an ointment, to treat skin problems:

1. **Issue/Requirement:** There is a need for a packaging supplier.
2. **Description of Needs:** It must be in the shape of a tube, rather than other shapes, such as a jar or a bottle.
3. **Requirements Specification:** 20 ml white aluminum tube with conical screw cap. Text must be printed directly on the tube.
4. **Supplier Search:** A pool of supplier options is selected in accordance to a set of criteria, i.e., image, location, size, financial soundness and just-in-time delivery.
5. **Qualification of Items:** Offer is given including price, payment and delivery terms, etc. The best three offers are selected.
6. **Supplier Selection:** The company visits the three best supplier candidates,

evaluates production conditions, and meets with the contact person(s). After a total assessment of steps 5 and 6, the company chooses the most suitable supplier.
7. **Selection of Delivery Terms, Payment, etc.:** The details are negotiated with the chosen supplier and formalized in a written agreement.
8. **Evaluation and Follow-up:** Product quality, delivery, and supplier cooperation are evaluated; invoices and delivery notes are checked, etc. Deviations and doubts are clarified, and minor adjustments are made.

HOW CAN YOU USE THE MODEL?

Firstly, the model gives an overall understanding of how a B2B purchase takes place and the significance of the purchase's novelty during the process.

Secondly, the model can be used to analyze each customer's unique purchase situation and what phases the customer goes through. This way, the marketing manager can adjust marketing efforts and the direction in which the messages are addressed.

For routine purchases, marketing efforts would be focused on nurturing customer relations in relation to direct sales, maintain top-of-mind communications, as well as maintain or develop product quality and attractive pricing.

For new purchases, marketing efforts are far more extensive, and it is crucial for the marketer to work from the beginning of the purchase process to be noticed as early in the process as possible, and to pull the customer's perception of needs and product specification towards the company's own products. It is important that the process continually identify potential suppliers and eliminates non-relevant ones so that, after steps 4 and 5, it becomes difficult or impossible to enter if you are not already among the selected.

Thirdly, the model can be used to segment. Buying situations are common segmentation criteria. Identical products will be a new purchase for some and a modified purchase for others, and some people may consider it a routine purchase.

WHAT ARE THE SHORTCOMINGS AND WEAKNESSES OF THE MODEL?

The model describes how the "customer" behaves, but not who the "customer" is. In B2B markets, the customer is part of a buying center that often includes a significant number of people, each with different roles and tasks. Moreover, the model does not include buying motives and only describes what the customer does but not why.

The model requires a rigorous, rational decision-making process and ignores that emotional aspects often influence behavior in practice. The behavior of B2B markets is, of course, primarily rational but not purely rational. Also, the process rarely does run in a linear manner, as the model describes. It is possible to revisit previous stages should something need to be re-evaluated, i.e., if new information is available, new decision makers enter, etc.

Finally, the purchase process is not an empty space, but is influenced by a number of factors both inside and outside the customer's business, for example, macro-environmental factors (see PESTEL, page 14), organizational factors, such as workflow, structure, culture, and technology, and relationships between the participants in the buying center, as well as the personal conditions of these individual participants. Personal conditions can include motives, work style, education, and internal status.

The model does not describe these very important aspects, and therefore, should not stand alone in detailing a given B2B market buying behavior.

REFERENCES

Andersen, Ole E., Svend Hollensen, Poul K. Faarup et al. (2016). *Moderne markedsføring*, 2nd edition. Copenhagen: Hans Reitzels Forlag.

Buch-Madsen, Kim (2005). *Marketing – klart og koncentreret*. Frederiksberg: Samfundslitteratur.

Hall, Simon (2017). *Innovative B2B Marketing: New Models, Processes and Theory*. London: Kogan Page Limited.

Jobber, David & Fiona Ellis-Chadwick (2016). *Principles and Practice of Marketing*, 8th edition. Maidenhead: McGraw-Hill Education.

Sarin, Sharad (2010). *Strategic Brand Management for B2B Markets: A Road Map for Organizational Transformation*. New Delhi: Sage Publications.

FCB-MODEL
By Ole E. Andersen

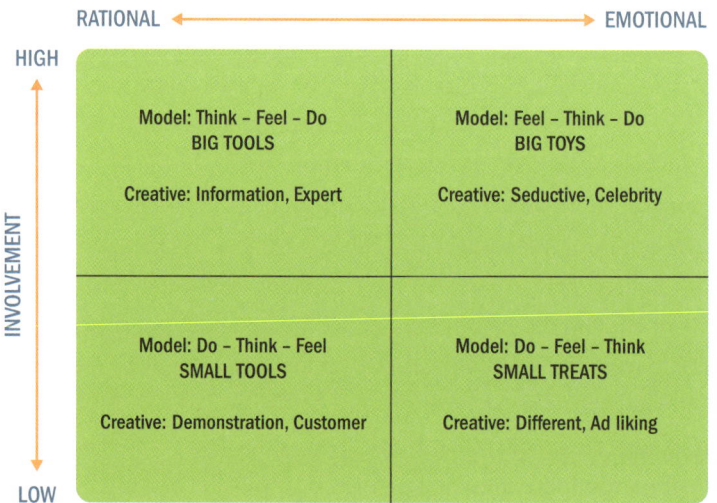

INTRODUCTION

This model classifies consumer/product relationships and decisions in two dimensions: the degree of involvement and rational-emotional considerations. The model provides guidelines for overall creative strategies.

WHAT IS THE MODEL ABOUT?

The FCB model is named after the American advertising agency Foote, Cone & Belding, where the strategic planner, Richard Vaughn, developed the model in 1980. The purpose was to be able to analyze how a product/service is perceived in the customer's mind in connection with a purchase decision.

Purchases are classified according to whether the customer is assumed to be highly or lowly involved and behave more rationally or emotionally in the decision-making process. Below are some examples of product categories in each of the four fields that result from a combination of the two dimensions:

- **Big tools:** mortgage, car battery, house insulation
- **Big toys:** holiday trips, fashion clothing, expensive perfumes/jewelry
- **Small tools:** mousetrap, detergent, headache pills, bread
- **Small treats:** chocolate, chips, lotto, beer, wine, movies, cafe.

Involvement expresses to what extent a consumer experiences risk, and devotes time and mental capacity, finding and evaluating products/brands. *Rationally-emotionally* demonstrates which factors are most prominent in the product decision-making process, evaluating whether logical thinking and consideration of a product's functional uses or emotions or psychological and emotional consequences have the biggest impact.

HOW CAN YOU USE THE MODEL?

The model, primarily developed for B2C markets, can be applied in three different ways for marketing. *First*, it can be used as an initial analysis and generate a discussion of where a given product category typically belongs based on insights into consumer decision-making. In the figure, each field has a model for the order in which the three components, theoretically, will occur: think, feel and do.

Second, the classification has implications for which overall creative strategy should be considered as a starting point. When buying a Big Tool, consumers need information and facts to make the decision, while considering a Big Toy is more influenced by visual and seductive stimuli. With Small Tools, demonstration of the product's USP (Unique Selling Proposition) is a relevant option, whereas creative strategy for Small Treats should be eye-catching, different, and "likable."

The *third* use is a specific dimension of creative strategy; which type of sender/endorser that will work best. For a Big Tool, an experienced expert will be relevant, while Big Toys will be better positioned with a celebrity (because the customer should be seduced). Small Tools should rely on a customer (as a testimonial) or an objective expert, while practically anything can work for Small Treats. It can be animals, celebrities, ordinary consumers or constructed characters for the campaign. As long as it's fun and feels good to see or hear.

WHAT ARE THE SHORTCOMINGS AND WEAKNESSES OF THE MODEL?

The model must always be used in relation to specific target groups, especially in terms of purchasing power. What might be a Small Treat for wealthy consumers (e.g., theater tickets), can be a Big Toy for target groups with less purchasing power, for example, students. The model lacks in that it does not take into consideration the *dynamics* primarily in many high involvement decisions in the form of a shift between rational and emotional views in different phases. Think of the decision to purchase an apartment can start rationally (price, size, year of construction), then switch to emotional considerations (nice, good, feel at home), and return to rational criteria (price, etc.).

A third weakness is there may be a big difference in classification in the *product category* or *brand* within the category. Good examples are computers where Mac is emotionally different, flights where Singapore Airlines have introduced emotional aspects or cars where the range goes from affordable means of transportation (e.g., Kia Picanto) to expensive brands, where design, status, prestige, and symbolic value are important elements (e.g., Audi).

Finally, it should be noted that the creative strategies mentioned, in particular, are only *guidelines* and not factual lists. Campaigns for primarily rationally-decided products may use emotional means to differentiate themselves in consumer awareness, but it is crucial for a decision to do so in a way that makes sense to the consumer.

REFERENCES

Andersen, Ole E. (2014). *Forstå forbrugerne og bliv en bedre markedsfører*. Frederiksberg: Samfundslitteratur.

Andersen, Ole E., Svend Hollensen, Poul K. Faarup et al. (2016). *Moderne markedsføring*, 2nd edition. Copenhagen: Hans Reitzels Forlag.

De Pelsmacker, Patrick, Maggie Geuens & Joeri Van den Bergh (2013). *Marketing Communications: A European Perspective*. 5th edition. Harlow: Pearson.

Fill, Chris & Sarah Turnbull (2016). *Marketing Communications*, 7th edition. Harlow: Pearson Education Limited.

Peter, J. Paul, Jerry C. Olson & Klaus G. Grunert (1999). *Consumer Behavior and Marketing Strategy: European Edition*. Berkshire: McGraw-Hill.

NET PROMOTER SCORE
By Ole E. Andersen

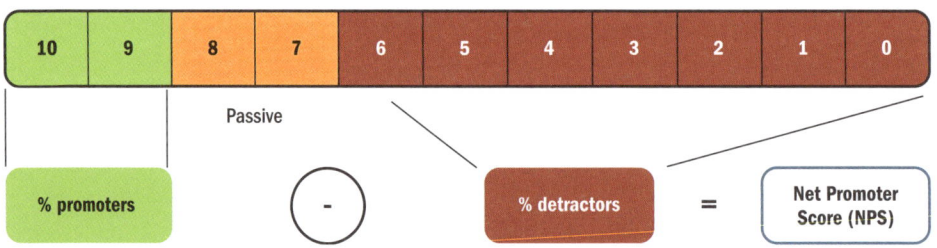

INTRODUCTION

The model is a quantitative analysis tool that, with response to a single question, gives a numeric score to a customer's overall assessment of a buying or visiting experience. It also indicates whether customers are promoters, passive or not satisfied.

WHAT IS THE MODEL ABOUT?

The Net Promoter Score (NPS) is essentially a measure of customer satisfaction; the model uses a customer's desire to recommend to people they know as an indicator of satisfaction. It can be part of a Customer Experience Management (CEM) program. This calculation is an important part of the NPS concept. You only group the *truly* positive and very satisfied customers (scale points 9 and 10) as "promoters," while all other customers who are somewhat or completely reluctant to give recommendations (grades 6 thru 0) are grouped as "detractors." People who answer 7 or 8 are predominantly positive but have some reservations, and therefore, are not included in the NPS calculation. In other words, you must have a great deal of very satisfied customers to earn a positive NPS score (see below).

HOW CAN YOU USE THE MODEL?

The model has especially gained ground as an online analysis tool for webshops, which register customers' email addresses in connection with purchases, or restaurants and theaters, which also register email addresses when clients order and book tickets online. The question in the NPS survey arises as an exit pop-up or a survey link sent via email immediately after the visit. The analysis does not have to be limited to buying or online activity. There may be people who have enrolled in a club, said yes to receive newsletters or otherwise provided their email address.

The question is what is a good or bad NPS? It depends on many factors, most importantly, industry and product category. The scoring can be outlined as follows:

NPS	- 100-0	1-49	50-100
General Evaluation	Bad	Fair/Good	Excellent

(The NPS score will be negative if there are more "detractors" than "promoters.")

The model can be used in all contact points with customers as a way for the company to continuously maximize enthusiastically satisfied customers and minimize customers who experience problems or where a company fails to meet customers' expectations fully.

The question of how likely the customer is to *recommend* the company or webshop to others is often accompanied by a comment box and an open question as to why the respondent holds the view just indicated in the questionnaire. It provides useful, qualitative input to explanations, although not everyone will answer and many answers will be quite short.

In conclusion, it should be emphasized the NPS concept can be used by any marketer regardless of industry. The questions can, of course, be part of a larger, more general market analysis based on, for example, telephone or face-to-face interviews.

WHAT ARE THE SHORTCOMINGS AND WEAKNESSES OF THE MODEL?

NPS is not an analysis you just execute once. The results must be measured continuously over time, taking into account changes to the website, product range, price levels, improved service, the introduction of live customer support via chat or other actions impacting customers. The individual company must at least have *internal* benchmarks and conduct its own measurements over time.

It would be even better to attain *external* benchmarks, such as comparisons with industry averages in that particular country, lowest and highest scores for the industry, and best of all, but difficult to obtain, the NPS for closest competitors. Even if a company has a great NPS, for example, 52, it is hardly good in the long run if the closest competitor has an NPS of 58.

Finally, it should be mentioned that when using NPS to send online questionnaires to customers or visitors, it is not possible to determine the response rate and, especially, who has responded. Is there an overrepresentation of dissatisfied customers or are there several relatively fully satisfied customers? If it can be assumed that possible overrepresentation is constant over time, this weakness is of less importance as it is still possible to compare NPS, e.g., month to month.

REFERENCES

Andersen, Ole E., Svend Hollensen, Poul K. Faarup et al. (2016). *Moderne markedsføring*, 2nd edition. Copenhagen: Hans Reitzels Forlag.

Chaffey, David & Fiona Ellis-Chadwick (2012). *Digital Marketing, Strategy, Implementation and Practice*, 5th edition. Harlow: Pearson Education Limited.

Net Promoter Network. *What is Net Promoter?* https://www.netpromoter.com/know (retrieved 01.03.17).

MARKETING RESEARCH PROCESS
By Ole E. Andersen

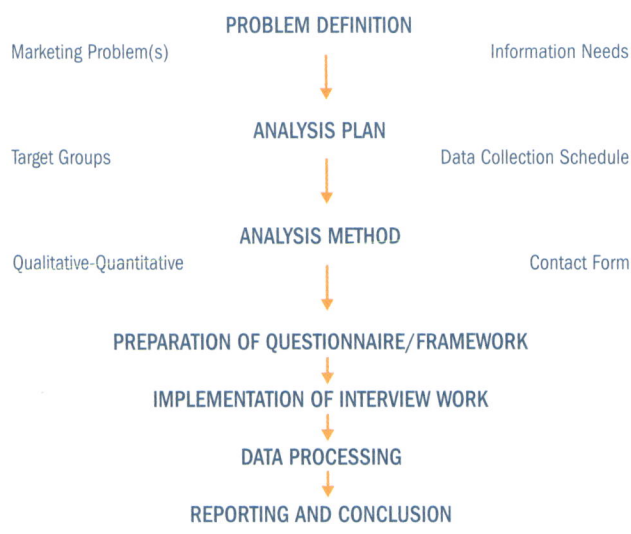

INTRODUCTION

The model demonstrates the phases that a market analysis process should ideally go through and in which order the sub-tasks must be solved to contribute to the decision-making platform for marketing activities.

WHAT IS THE MODEL ABOUT?

The model illustrates the logical process that should be performed prior to primary data collection, i.e., market analyses to investigate an identified marketing problem. Problems could include decreasing sales, fewer loyal customers, declining brand awareness or less customer satisfaction. In the more positive aspect of the issues, it may be testing a new product or name or general annual measurement of own and competing brands/organizations' image among the population or in target groups. The three core phases of the process are analysis plan, analytical method, and reporting and conclusion.

Analysis Plan: Who should be questioned and when are the two sub-issues that need to be addressed. As to *whom*, it can be a well-known and well-defined target group, i.e., in terms of demography, geography, and lifestyle. It may also be interesting to ask a slightly broader group to look at the feedback and response of people who could become potential buyers or customers.

Regarding *when* data collection should occur, it is important to be aware of 1) predictable events affecting respondents' interest and response patterns, such as holidays, elections and payday, and 2) time fluctuations in consumption during the week, month or season. For example, all households buy significantly more food and groceries up to holidays like Christmas, Easter, and Thanksgiving, and they exercise much more in the first three months than the rest of the year. In general, it is about getting results that reflect a "normal" period/condition on the market.

Analysis Method: First, it deals with the decision on quantitative and/or qualitative analysis which serves different purposes. The *quantitative* analysis with many respondents aims to generalize from a sample to the entire population/target group. It identifies the wide majority, for example, the percentage who know or purchase a brand. When using quantitative methods, *contact form* must be decided, i.e., how respondents should be interviewed. It can be face-to-face/personal interviews at residences, the workplace or on the street, telephone interviews or the most widely used: online or web surveys. *Qualitative* analysis has few respondents but goes into more detail and gives a holistic picture of the respondents' mental map of the subject in question.

Reporting and conclusion: This phase is the most important phase of the analysis process. After the technical analysis is completed, the marketer should have answers for all relevant questions and sufficient information to provide a solid foundation for decision making. It is important the report is not a boring collection of numbers or quotes. It must be structured and written to cover the marketing problem and the analysis's response to the relevant information needs (Phase 1).

HOW CAN YOU USE THE MODEL?

The model indicates the sub-tasks in an analysis process and the order in which they are best solved. This process ensures that the investment in a market analysis provides the optimal return and the most useful and operational results for a particular issue. One of the most common mistakes occurs when companies decide on the analysis plan and method *before* systematically evaluating what information is needed and what marketing issue it wants to address.

In the *qualitative* analysis method, there is a tendency to choose focus groups without sufficient consideration of other qualitative methods. It must be the actual problem and information need that determine whether focus groups or, for example, in-depth interviews (with a few individuals) are the right solution. In this context, emphasis should be placed on whether the projective techniques that facilitate dialogue on more unconscious aspects of respondents' feelings for a product, brand or situation will accurately depict the subject.

WHAT ARE THE SHORTCOMINGS AND WEAKNESSES OF THE MODEL?

Unlike other models for marketing analysis planning, the model lacks a *budget* phase. This is because it describes the *optimal* process where the problem statement or the issue alone is indicative of what should be the "right" market analysis, and not what is budgeted for the analysis. The latter, however, occurs often in the real world.

Another weakness of the model is that the ideal analysis process can cause a critical delay in both decision making and concrete subsequent marketing activities in dynamic markets with intense competition. Here, fast actions are often required, and a compromise must be made between time, pressure, security, and in-depth results.

Finally, it should be mentioned, typical analytical problems that commonly occur at a more detailed level are not explicitly embraced by the model. For example, this applies to the selection and size of the sample, as well as the concrete design of questions and structure in the questionnaire for quantitative analyses. These tasks are often assigned to professional analysis firms to ensure valid and reliable measurements of the desired variables.

REFERENCES

Andersen, Ole E., Svend Hollensen, Poul K. Faarup et al. (2016). *Moderne markedsføring*, 2nd edition. Copenhagen: Hans Reitzels Forlag.

Gordon, Wendy & Roy Longmaid (1988). *Qualitative Market Research*. Aldershot: Gower Publishing.

Kotler, Philip T., Kevin Lane Keller, Mairead Brady et al. (2016). *Marketing Management*. 3rd edition. Harlow: Pearson Education Limited.

2. MARKETING MIX AND VALUE PACK

8 P (MARKETING MIX)
By Ole E. Andersen

Product
Variety
Quality/design
Brand name
Features
Packaging
Warranty
Returns

Price
Price list
Credit terms
Discounts

Promotion
Advertising offline and online
SEM/search engines
Social media/blogs
Sponsorships and events
Word-of-Mouth (WOM)
Public relations
Sales promotion
Direct marketing

Policy
Corporate Social
  Responsibility (CSR)
Working conditions
Environmental awareness
Sustainability
Decent behavior

Place (distribution)
Channels
Logistics
Locations
Dealers
Webshop
Branches

Physical evidence
Facilities
Inventory
Sound/light, smell, taste
Cars/trucks
Uniforms

Processes
Customer service
Company culture
Databases
Service manuals
Self-service

People
Employees
Recruitment
Education
Internal marketing
Service-oriented

INTRODUCTION

The model demonstrates the action parameters in the marketer's toolbox, i.e., the buttons that can be adjusted to achieve set goals or solve problems in the market.

WHAT IS THE MODEL ABOUT?

The Marketing Mix is a structural breakdown of the focus areas a marketer can address or adjust when entering a new market or in response to a given situation.

The history of the P model reflects increasing competition, changed market terms and conditions, along with growth in the service industry. From the classic 4 Ps back in the 1960s (Product, Price, Place, and Promotion) to the 5 Ps with 'People' as an independent action parameter to the 2000s which saw the addition of 'Physical Evidence' and 'Processes,' both particularly important to service companies. The newest P, Policy, reflects customers' increasing awareness of how products are made and companies' awareness of e.g. pollution. Companies must have a Corporate Social Responsibility (CSR) policy.

HOW CAN YOU USE THE MODEL?

When the overall strategy and the desired positioning are determined, it is in the composition of the Marketing Mix that the company must develop, communicate, and deliver value to the defined target groups. The P model can thus be used by a new company or startup as inspiration and guidance for market activities when introducing products or services.

All Ps must be viewed collectively so that customers will experience a harmonized effort, whereby the product is need-satisfying, reasonably priced, accessible to customers and, finally, communicated clearly, and consistently across different media platforms.

For established companies and brands, the P model can be used as a checklist for ongoing marketing adjustments either proactively to be ahead of competitors, and market trends, or reactively by changing elements of the Marketing Mix in the situation where goals have not been met.

Finally, the P model is a good analytical framework for describing a company's marketing activities in study assignments or practice, as it can be used to analyze the Marketing Mix of an individual company or that of its competitors.

WHAT ARE THE SHORTCOMINGS AND WEAKNESSES OF THE MODEL?

The largest criticism of the model is that it is outdated and conceived in an era without digital technology, internet access, social media, globalization, network economics, etc. It does not demonstrate that the consumer is in the "driver's seat."

This criticism is unjustified though. Regardless of the market's complexity, dynamics and digital development, the marketer will always be the ultimate decision maker for market activities. It is still called "marketing management," even though the challenges in solving the tasks have been multiplied, especially with increasing digitization.

All companies find themselves in a more complex world with greater competition and customers who focus on one thing: "What is the value for me?" As a result, another weakness of the 8 P model is that when viewed alone, the model is introverted and can cause companies to determine the action parameters without consideration for near or distant external factors.

To counteract this "producer orientation," the 4 C model has been developed to evaluate the standard action parameters from the customer's point of view:

- **The product** must create value for the customer: Customer value.
- **The price** is a cost to the customer: Cost.
- **Place** – it should be easy for the customer to access: Convenience.
- **Promotion** should be elements of good conversations: Conversations.

One can argue the model should include a ninth P, Partnerships, as it is increasingly important to associate with other companies to gain strength in the competition. It may be suppliers, intermediaries or companies from different industries that, together, can create stronger products and services.

REFERENCES

Andersen, Finn Rolighed, Bjarne Warming Jensen, Mette Risgaard Olsen et al. (2015). *International markedsføring*, 5th edition. Copenhagen: Trojka.

Andersen, Ole E., Svend Hollensen, Poul K. Faarup et al. (2016). *Moderne markedsføring*, 2nd edition. Copenhagen: Hans Reitzels Forlag.

Fahy, John & David Jobber (2015). *Foundations of Marketing*, 5th edition. London: McGraw-Hill Education.

Kotler, Philip T., Kevin Lane Keller, Mairead Brady et al. (2016). *Marketing Management*, 3rd edition. Harlow: Pearson Education Limited.

THE FIVE PRODUCT DIMENSIONS
By Birgitte W. Grandjean

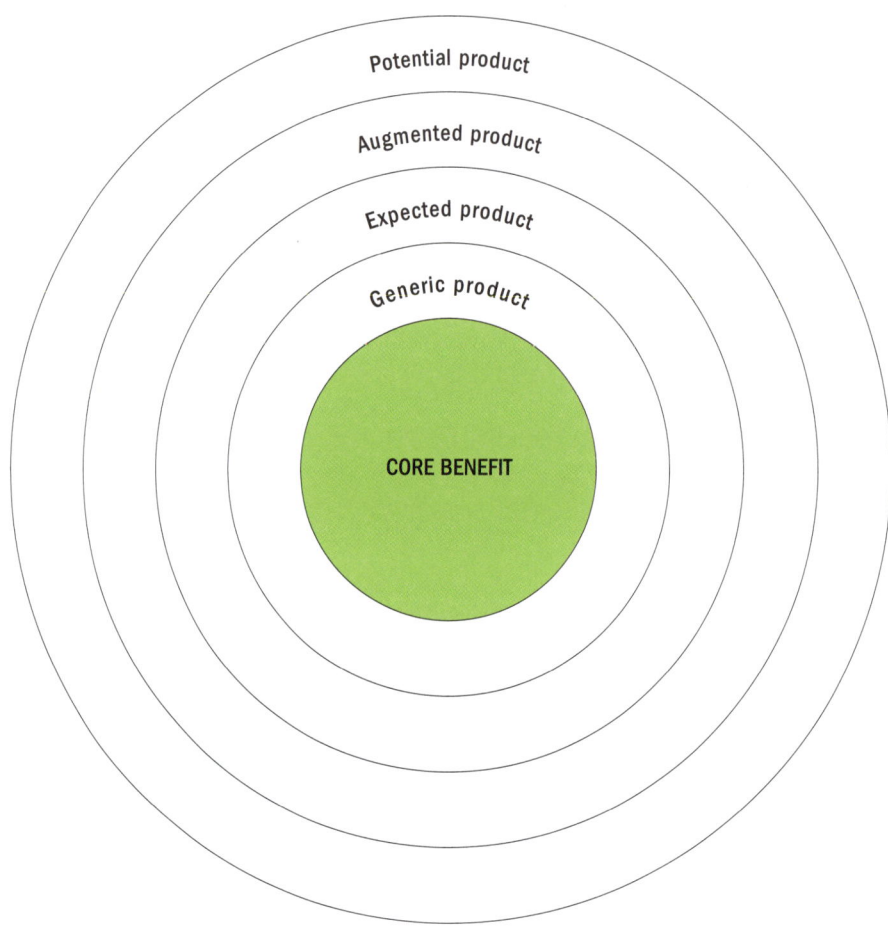

INTRODUCTION

The model is used to identify all the values that customers attach to a product or could add to it in the future.

WHAT IS THE MODEL ABOUT?

A product is more than a specific "thing," or a "service." A product, as a starting point, covers a customer's specific needs. However, the product does not just consist of this *specific* value. The product is also associated with an *abstract* value of great importance as to whether the customer purchases the product. Thus, customers choose a product based on the overall value perception.

Kotler's Five Product Level model operates within five product dimensions that describe how the company links various additional dimensions to a product to optimize customers' overall value perception. The product dimensions describe how the company attempts to accommodate to customers different needs based upon the company's market knowledge. The model covers, among other things, the functional and emotional needs the product provides:

- **Core benefit:** The basic need the customer wishes to satisfy with a service or product. For example, the need for an item to protect the body from the weather conditions: a piece of warm clothing that keeps the rain and cold out.
- **Generic product:** A basic version of the product with only the essential features for the product to function. For example, a coat with a satisfactory fit, made of a material that can keep one warm and dry, as well as a mechanism that ensures the coat can be closed.
- **Expected product:** Here, the focus is on all the features customers normally expect to receive when purchasing a given product. For example, the coat is of a durable quality that can withstand cleaning but is also comfortable to wear, allowing you to move freely.
- **Augmented product:** Includes all the additional factors that differentiate the product from competitors' similar offers. They are the product's special advantages that reinforce its positive value. Brand identity and image will often play an important role in how products are perceived and assessed by customers. Also, product guarantees and services directly related to the product, such as customer support 24/7, fall into this category.

- **Potential product:** To ensure future customer loyalty and competitiveness, a company should surprise and please its customers. Potential benefits are those elements that are not part of the product but could be. It is largely regarding opportunities for product development and innovation. In the coat example, there might be the possibility of a personal shopper when investing in a new coat, or access to an entire lifestyle universe, where the values and interests the product brand represents, can be shared.

HOW CAN YOU USE THE MODEL?

The model is a proven method of structuring a customer's product experience. The model can be used, for example, to define a product strategy, develop a concept, or analyze competitors' products.

The model demonstrates how a company, by looking at the product, nuanced with multiple product dimensions, can add value-increasing factors to the product. Each of the five product dimensions adds value to the customer. The greater the effort a company makes on each of the five levels, the more likely it is that the company and its products will be perceived as differentiated and as something unique that customers are willing to pay extra for.

In short, it is not just about satisfying customers, but also about exceeding their expectations and surprising them. By thinking creatively and using relevant customer insight, differentiated customer experiences and a unique overall value experience can be created for the customer using systematically all of the model's product's dimensions.

WHAT ARE THE SHORTCOMINGS AND WEAKNESSES OF THE MODEL?

It is usually easy to describe the core and generic benefits of a product. Conversely, it may be more difficult to identify and describe the factors beyond the product. It can be anything from a preference for the company or the product image to the "taste" or a certain sense of the experienced service associated with the purchase of the product. It is important to think holistically and in the context of the product when analyzing customer needs in product dimensions.

It is also important to note the model should be used to describe the factors customers experience. Make sure you have real customer insight – and be careful not to describe what you *think* they are experiencing.

The model does not include which differentiation strategy the company follows. Is the focus on low cost or unique differentiating sides of the product? This will greatly influence what elements the company will build into the product and how many, as well as how these are specifically designed. Read more about differentiation in Porter's Competitive Strategies.

REFERENCES

Andersen, Ole E., Svend Hollensen, Poul K. Faarup et al. (2016). *Moderne markedsføring*, 2nd edition. Copenhagen: Hans Reitzels Forlag.

Doyle, Peter (2008). *Value-based Marketing: Marketing Strategies for Corporate Growth and Shareholder Value,* 2nd edition. Hoboken: John Wiley & Sons.

Kotler, Philip T., Kevin Lane Keller, Mairead Brady et al. (2009). *Marketing Management.* Upper Saddle River: Pearson/Prentice Hall.

SERVICE TRIANGLE
By Kim Buch-Madsen

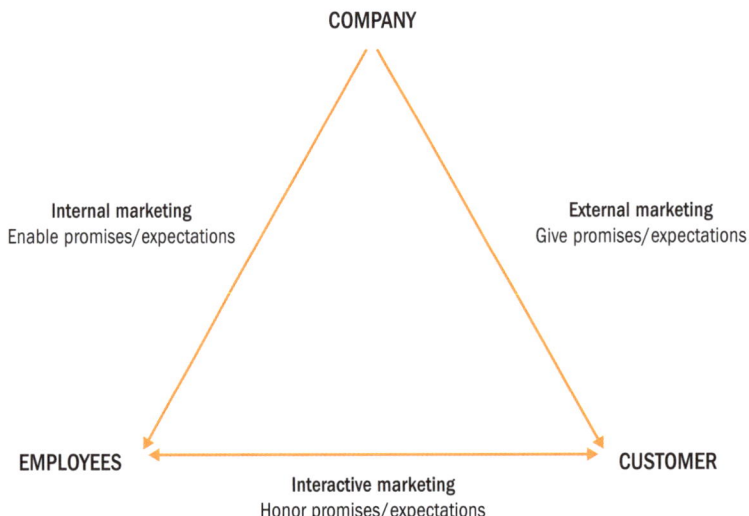

INTRODUCTION

This model demonstrates the three dimensions of marketing of services and how they relate to each other. In addition, the model shows marketing of services in a broader context, giving importance to both the customer's direct interaction with front staff and the company's training of front staff for this crucial meeting.

WHAT IS THE MODEL ABOUT?

The model is about incorporating the two additional dimensions that the marketing of services implicate, linking them with traditional marketing ("external marketing"), and ensuring that the three elements tie together and pull in the same direction.

External marketing is the traditional activity of a marketing mix, primarily Price, Place, Promotion and Product. This part of marketing creates the promise made to the customer, which is expected to be met in interactions with the front employee, and thereby the expectations that must be fulfilled in order for the customer to feel satisfied and experience quality service.

Interactive marketing is the direct exchange between the customer and front staff, who must meet customer expectations in order for the customer to experience good quality service. This is the most important part of the marketing of services and so crucial that it is called the "moment of truth." It is called this because the service delivery is more or less created in the interaction between the customer and the front employee, and this meeting becomes the core of the service for which the customer has paid.

Internal marketing is about recruiting and training front staff who are good at meeting customer expectations and who can handle the human interaction that is essential for good service. Internal marketing is also about informing, training, and motivating front staff, so they are capable of delivering the core service that customers expect and are motivated to give customers the little extra something that can make a big difference – especially in services, which depend on human interaction. Information and training can, for example, ensure that front employees are well-informed about specific and current campaigns, and they are trained to understand the company's strategy, values, positioning, etc., so they treat customers according to what the company represents.

HOW CAN YOU USE THE MODEL?

The model can be used to ensure that service marketing takes place in the broad context that quality service requires, and through internal marketing also involves activities that are usually considered as Human Resources (HR) work. In addition, the model demonstrates how the most important part of companies' service marketing takes place in the direct meeting between the customer and front desk worker, where the core of service is delivered via human interaction, as illustrated by the double arrow in the model. Finally, the model demonstrates which contexts should be managed to ensure service quality and, thereby, customer satisfaction. Namely, external marketing should build up the expectations with which a customer enters a business and internal marketing should ensure the front worker's ability and motivation to meet those expectations in the absolutely crucial "moment of truth."

WHAT ARE THE SHORTCOMINGS AND WEAKNESSES OF THE MODEL?

The model is a conceptual model and a good framework that outlines the three types of marketing that must be closely tied together in effective service marketing. However, the model does not address how to ensure this correlation. For example, it does not provide guidelines for how to create effective internal marketing or what constitutes good interactive marketing in the "moment of truth." The model does not include the physical elements of services, such as the decoration of a hotel room that can significantly affect the service experience, or the service delivery system, which can also be very important. In hotels, for example, the service delivery systems include systems for booking and cleaning rooms. These activities take place before and after the actual delivery of the core service.

Finally, the model does not distinguish between different service levels, as the service theory does, because there are service elements in virtually all products. Therefore, the model will best suit service offerings with a high level of service and the greater the physical part, the weaker the relevance of the model.

REFERENCES

Buch-Madsen, Kim (2005). *Marketing – klart og koncentreret*. Frederiksberg: Samfundslitteratur.

Hatcher, Andrew (2015). *Cambridge Marketing Handbook: Services Marketing*. Cambridge: Cambridge Marketing Press.

Jobber, David & Fiona Ellis-Chadwick (2016). *Principles and Practice of Marketing*, 8th edition. Maidenhead: McGraw-Hill Education.

Zeithaml, Valarie A., Mary Jo Bitner, Dwayne D. Gremler (2017) *Services Marketing*, 7th edition. New York: McGraw-Hill Education.

CUSTOMER VALUE
By Kim Buch-Madsen

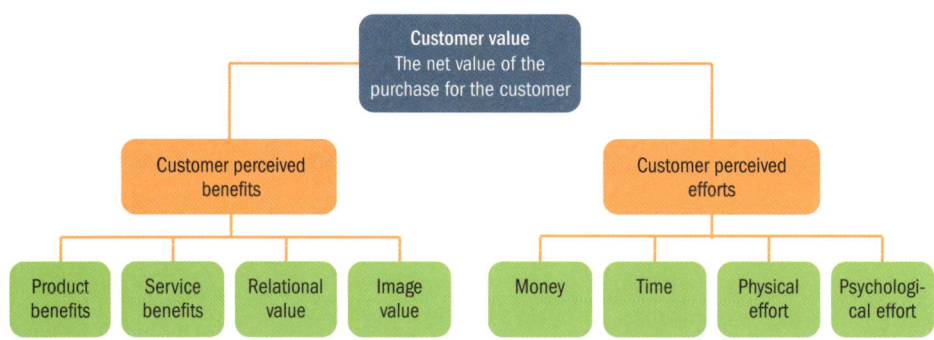

INTRODUCTION

The model demonstrates the main elements that are included in a customer's perceived value, and which determine whether a customer purchases or not. The left side indicates the benefits a customer experiences when buying, and the right side is the experienced effort. The company can influence a customer to purchase, either by adding to the customer's perceived benefit or by removing something from the customer's perceived efforts.

WHAT IS THE MODEL ABOUT?

When a customer decides to purchase a product, the decision is based on whether the customer experiences the benefits to be greater than the effort it requires for a customer to buy.

The model describes which key elements are included in this "internal calculation" that a customer systematically and consciously goes through before certain purchases and quickly, intuitively and unconsciously for other purchases.

The customer's trade-off of experienced benefits and effort are subjective and can be influenced by the company utilizing the marketing mix, see the 8 P model, page 56.

The model describes four different types of "benefits" and four different types of "effort." These are both solid things such as product characteristics, money, and abstract relationships, such as personal relationships or psychological efforts.

The four forms of "perceived benefit" are:

- **Product Benefits:** Specific Product Features, Quality Level, Design, etc. When buying clothes, for example, it could be design, fashion, fit and durability.
- **Service Benefits:** The service elements included. There may be specific elements such as exchange service or an exclusive canvas bag to transport the clothes home. There can also be abstract elements such as a salesperson's knowledge and know-how about the products.
- **Relational Value:** Most purchases are made through human interaction, even for online purchases, as many providers have a real-time chat function whereby one can ask a real person for advice. A good relationship with staff or a specific agent can be essential to a customer's perceived benefit.
- **Image Value:** Finally, the image of the company or brand may have an impact

on a customer's decision to make a purchase. For example, in the clothing industry, it may include both the product brand and the image of the store or chain.

The four forms of "experienced effort" are:

- **Money:** The price of the item and other costs associated with the purchase. Particularly for B2B products, there may be many other costs involved than just the price, such as financing or maintenance expenses. For clothing purchases, the customer will typically consider both the actual price and discount options of the clothing, if there is a sale coming up, etc.
- **Time:** Every purchase takes time, and a customer wants to minimize that time unless the purchase itself is a significant part of the experience, as it is often seen when shopping for clothing. The customer's investment of time includes research before the purchase, for example on the internet, and the time the purchase takes. In the case of clothing purchases, not enough store employees can result in a long wait and cause the customer to choose another store. When buying online, a customer is often very sensitive to slow payment processing, which can quickly cause the customer to cancel the purchase.
- **Physical Action:** Where and how the purchase actually takes place and how far the customer is willing to drive to go to the store plays a role too. In general, convenience is important to many purchases and is the basis for many e-business concepts. When purchasing clothing on the internet, a customer can both shop and buy without leaving the house.
- **Psychological Effort:** The psychological effort can influence in numerous ways. For example, a customer always experiences risks when making a purchase. Would I regret it, does it work, can I afford it, what do other people think? See the perceived risk model, page 22. The purchase decision itself that is the comparison with alternative products, understanding the actual price, etc., is also a psychological effort that can be minimized, for example, by simplified products and price structure. For example, when customers purchase clothing, they may encounter risks such as "Does the expensive dress fit my wardrobe?" or "Will my boyfriend like it?" or "Is it hot or not?" In the clothing industry, efforts are made to simplify the psychological effort in the purchase decision when offering sales such as "All on this shelf for price X" or "40 % discount on all products."

HOW CAN YOU USE THE MODEL?

In any purchase, a customer attempts to achieve or avoid something. This model can be used to understand what the customer desires to maximize (benefit) and minimize (effort) when purchasing a product or service. The model also demonstrates the need to look beyond the core product or service when the company attempts to understand what motivates the customer to purchase or not.

In addition, the model demonstrates the factors that a company can influence through its marketing to create value for the customer and instigate a purchase, either by adding something to the customer's benefit or by reducing the customer's efforts. The model can also be used to develop new products or services and inspire ideas for where and how the company can add value to the customer.

Analytically, the model can be used to examine what is important to customers, and how the company's performance is compared to its competitors as seen from the consumer's perspective. Similarly, the model can be utilized to analyze the composition of a competitor's performance in the customer's perspective.

Finally, the model can be used to diagnose the possible reasons that sales are not as expected. Is "experienced benefit" too low? Where and how? Is "experienced effort" too high? Where and how?

WHAT ARE THE SHORTCOMINGS AND WEAKNESSES OF THE MODEL?

Generally, the model gives a fair overview. The lower boxes of the model demonstrate benefits and efforts but are still fairly general. Applying the model requires the benefits and efforts to be specified in relation to the situation. Headings such as "Product Benefits," "Image Value," "Time," and "Psychological Efforts" can cover many complex issues that typically require analysis of customer data or actual market research.

The model only demonstrates which benefits and efforts the company can influence in its marketing but not how.

Finally, the model presents the individual factors without weighing the importance of each factor to the customer. In practice, they will typically be of widely different importance depending upon the specific service and target group.

REFERENCES

Buch-Madsen, Kim (2006). *Hvad er marketing?* Kursuskompendium. Copenhagen: IBC Euroforum.

Jobber, David & Fiona Ellis-Chadwick (2016). *Principles and Practice of Marketing*, 8th edition. Maidenhead: McGraw-Hill Education.

Kotler, Philip T., Kevin Lane Keller, Mairead Brady et al. (2009). *Marketing Management*. Upper Saddle River: Pearson/Prentice Hall.

VALUE PROPOSITION CANVAS
By Jan Kyhnau

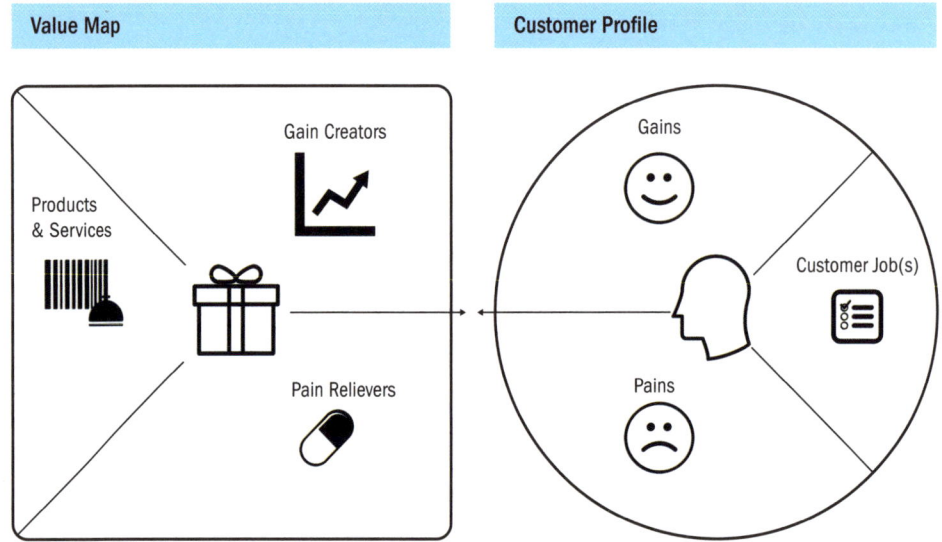

INTRODUCTION

Alexander Osterwalder's Value Proposition Canvas (VPC) helps companies develop products and services customers actually want.

The model zooms in on the two basic building blocks of the Business Model Canvas: *Customer Segments* and *Value Propositions*, and outlines the intersection between customer needs and the company's ability to meet them. The model reveals gaps, highlighting needed improvements or innovations.

WHAT IS THE MODEL ABOUT?

The VPC is a strategic management tool designed for companies to visualize, design, and test a business model's value offering to its customers. The model was developed by Alexander Osterwalder and his team in connection with their work with the Business Model Canvas (see page 166). It thoroughly investigates the two basic building blocks of *Customer Segments* and *Value Propositions*, which together comprise the DNA of a business model.

The idea behind the model is that it should clarify the relationship between a customer segment's conscious and unconscious needs and the real value the company creates and delivers through its business model. While the Business Model Canvas shows how value is created for the company, the VPC shows how value is created for customers.

The VPC consists of two parts: *Customer Profile* on one hand and *Value Map* on the other. Each part consists of three building blocks which, together, illustrate the customer's needs and the company's value offering. The better match or "fit," as Osterwalder calls it, there is between the two sides of the model, the bigger creation of real value for the customers. In other words, the VPC demonstrates the probability of whether a company's products and services will either succeed or fail.

Customer Profile describes the customer perspective through three building blocks:

1. **Customer Jobs** describe the tasks customers want to solve in connection with a concrete situation or performance in their private life or at work. Jobs can be functional, social or personal/emotional.

2. **Pains** describe the negative factors that make it difficult or prevent customers from getting their jobs done. Pains can be concrete barriers, frustrations or negative situations one hopes to avoid or ease/minimize.
3. **Gains** describe the positive factors and benefits gained when customers get their jobs done. Gains may be the achievement of basic, expected, desired or unexpected benefits.

Value Map describes the company's value offerings through three building blocks:

1. **Products & Services** include a list of the specific products and services a company offers to help customers get their jobs done. Products & Services can be either tangible, intangible, digital or financial.
2. **Pain Relievers** describe how concrete products and services relieve customers' pain by either reducing or eliminating the pain. Pain Relievers can be savings (time, money), elimination of risks or breakdown of barriers that prevent happiness and well-being.
3. **Gain Creators** describe how products or services create, improve or maximize the benefits customers expect, want or will be surprised to get. Gain Creators can lead to functional, economic, social, and emotional benefits.

Like the Business Model Canvas, the VPC is thought of as a dynamic team tool that emphasizes visualization and interaction, e.g., through the use of colored sticky notes.

HOW CAN YOU USE THE MODEL?

Generally, the VPC is used to create crystal clear propositions as the focal point for successful business models. The model can be utilized to analyze value propositions in existing business models but is particularly effective in innovative processes, where the purpose is visualizing, designing, and testing the value-creating factors that are meaningful to customers.

The model can serve as an independent tool but is often used in strategic business development based on the Business Model Canvas. The VPC is an easy-to-use, manageable tool that can be employed by startups to create a value offer from scratch, as well as existing companies wishing to optimize or innovate their value propositions and business model. The model can be used in relation to both the company's total portfolio of value propositions and individual value propositions.

In project studies, the model, among other things, can be used to describe the DNA in a company's business model and to analyze the connection between value propositions and customer behavior. In addition, the model can be used in combination with competitor analysis and/or comparisons, as well as part of work on segmentation, targeting and positioning.

Essentially, the VPC is thought of as an iterative development tool, where you can quickly generate multiple variants of value propositions – prototypes – which can be tested against each other.

WHAT ARE THE SHORTCOMINGS AND WEAKNESSES OF THE MODEL?

By itself, the VPC model is very simple and provides, without research, data collection, testing, and validation – only an indication of which value propositions may be relevant for a business to invest in. The simplicity of the model might lead many to perceive it as a superficial mechanism, without real value as a strategic management tool.

However, it would be unjust to Alexander Osterwalder to not correct this presumption. He specifically points out that the VPC only has value if the model is used to summarize the insights collected through thorough research and repeated use of hypothesis-based testing and validation of data. The canvas is merely a practical tool that provides a summary of underlying calculations and results of the analyses, as well as the structure and direction of a company's work to invent or reinvent itself.

Just like in his first book, *Business Model Generation*, the emphasis is placed on making the model accessible to more people by creating a common language and a common "game board" for developing a company's value propositions. Based on the notion that more minds think better than a few, the number of ideas developed, determine the quality of the idea and value proposition with which you end up.

REFERENCES

Andersen, Ole E., Svend Hollensen, Poul K. Faarup et al. (2016). *Moderne markedsføring*, 2nd edition. Copenhagen: Hans Reitzels Forlag.

Kyhnau, Jan & Christian Nielsen (2015). Value Proposition Design: From the practitioner's and the professor's point of view. *Journal of Business Models*, 3 (1): 81-92.

Osterwalder, Alexander & Yves Pigneur (2010). *Business Model Generation: A Handbook for Visionaries, Game Changers and Challengers*. Hoboken: John Wiley & Sons.

Osterwalder, Alexander, Yves Pigneur, Greg Bernarda et al. (2010). *Value Proposition Design: How to Create Products and Services Customers Want*. Hoboken: John Wiley & Sons. https://strategyzer.com/canvas.

AAKER'S BRAND IDENTITY PLANNING MODEL
By Heidi Hansen

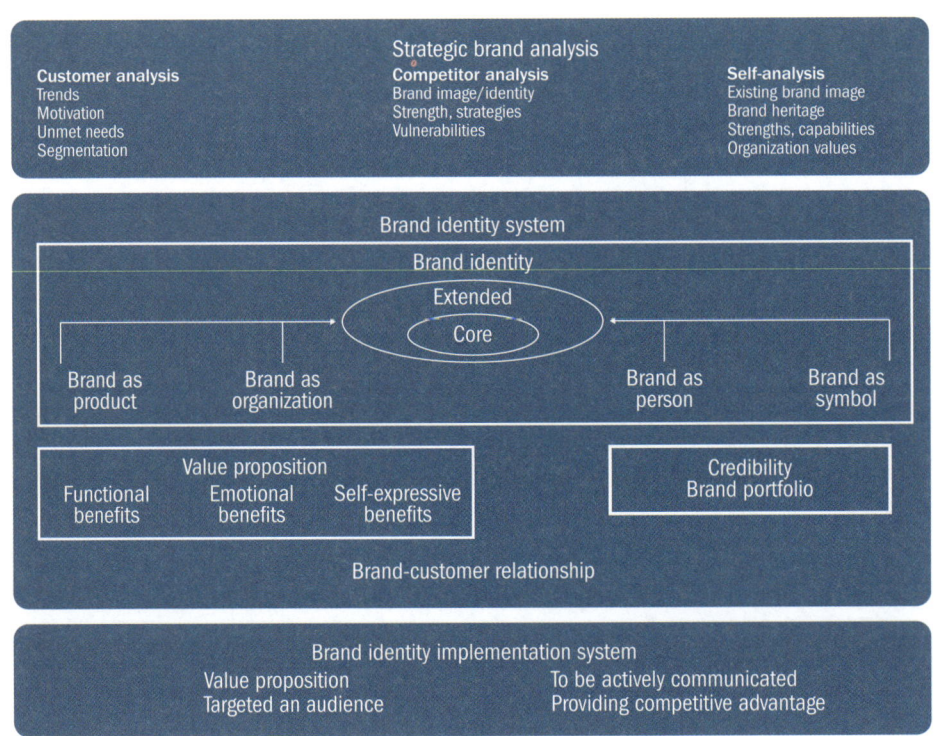

INTRODUCTION

David Aaker's Brand Identity Planning Model offers a framework for brand analysis. The model provides an overview of key aspects, a company ought to consider and evaluate when choosing and designing brand strategies.

WHAT IS THE MODEL ABOUT?

Aaker's Brand Identity Planning Model aims at outlining the numerous considerations one ought to make in designing and evaluating brand strategies. Aaker pinpoints that many brands fail because they are conceptualized too narrowly, and the identity planning model has been developed to assist the strategist consider the brand from different perspectives, thus gaining an overview of brand elements as well as threats and opportunities. The Brand Identity Planning Model is divided into three overall categories. The first category is called *strategic brand analysis,* and the aim of this part of the analysis is to uncover market factors such as market segments, consumer behavior, competitors, and organizational strengths and vulnerabilities. The next part of the analysis – *brand identity system* – is designed to undertake an in-depth analysis of the product and the immaterial brand value in order to design an appealing brand identity. The final part of the analysis – *brand identity implementation system* – relates to the marketing of the brand. The purpose of the Brand Identity Planning Model is to broaden the brand concept to include more than product attributes and existing brand image. To develop a strong brand identity, one must include more dimensions and perspectives and brainstorm on all of the possible brand elements mentioned in the model.

The *strategic brand analysis* embraces three sub-themes: customer analysis, competitor analysis, and self-analysis. In the *customer analysis*, one considers which prospective customers (market segments) the brand may appeal to. Oftentimes, the target group is not decided by the physical product attributes but rather by packaging, emotional values, and the brand universe that is built around the product. All of these latter aspects are something that is decided by the brand strategist, and therefore the strategist ought to consider unmet needs, trends and buying motive in relation to different target groups. The aim of the *competitor analysis* is to identify primary and secondary competitors. However, it is important to notice that these competitors will differ according to which target group and value proposition one considers. The *self-analysis* evaluates the company behind the product. The aim is to uncover strengths and weaknesses and to identify whether the new brand ought to be linked to an existing brand heritage or whether it should be marketed independently. Cf. the *Brand Architecture* model, the association between the corporate brand and the sub-brand can be strong or weak.

Having analyzed markets factors, one ought to undertake a detailed brand analysis. The *brand identity system* considers the brand as product, organization, person and symbol. The *brand as product* considers product-related associations such as functional benefits and utilization. The *brand as organization* considers organizational attributes such as culture, values and corporate social responsibility (CSR) for instance. Organizational attributes provide long-lasting competitive advantage compared to functional product benefits that may easily be imitated by competitors. Inspired by theory about brand personality and brand-consumer relationships, the purpose of *brand as person* is to identify a desirable brand personality seeing that brand personality can create a relationship between the customer and the brand. The *brand as symbol* considers how to represent the brand by use of signs as well as the symbolic value that signs may contribute to the brand.

Based on the four sub-themes in the brand identity system and the strategic brand analysis a brand identity, consisting of a core and an extended identity, can now be coined. The brand identity determines the brand's *value proposition*. A value proposition is a statement of the functional, emotional, and self-expressive benefits offered by the brand to be used by the consumer in his or her staging of self. In the construction of brand identity, *credibility* of the brand portfolio is an issue to consider. As showcased by the Brand Architecture model, a company may choose from a number of different branding strategies according to how a new sub-brand fits the existing Brand Architecture.

Finally, the *brand identity implementation system* is used to develop a marketing plan for the brand.

HOW CAN YOU USE THE MODEL?

The Brand Identity Planning Model is a framework that outlines a number of brand elements that can help clarify, enrich, and differentiate a brand identity. The model can be applied to *develop new brands* to ensure that brand decisions are based in strategic analyses. The model may also be used to *re position* an existing brand. The reasons why a company looks to re-position its brand may vary, but it is often related to failing sales and loss of market share. Finally, the Brand Identity Planning Model can be applied in a *strategic revision of the brand*. Many brands are developed on the basis of a good idea, and initial decisions are a result of a moment of creativity rather than strategic analysis. In this case, the Brand Identity Planning Model can spur a systematic approach to the brand creation process.

WHAT ARE THE SHORTCOMINGS AND WEAKNESSES OF THE MODEL?

The Brand Identity Planning Model provides a comprehensive framework for the brand strategist. It is a very ambitious model that presupposes a basic theoretical knowledge about market analysis, competitor analysis, consumer behavior, brand personality and marketing planning – in addition to access to market data. The various analyses can be strengthened by use of such theories that provide specialized insight. The customer analysis may be complemented by theories of needs and demands such as Maslow or theories about values, lifestyle and consumer behavior. The competitor analysis may be complemented by Porter's generic strategies and Five Forces, or competitive position (leader, follower, challenger, niche position), and the self-analysis may be complemented by organization theory. The analysis of brand identity system may be complemented by theories about purchase decision process, user, buyer, group influence, and opinion leaders.

Applying the Brand Identity Planning Model is laborious and time-consuming. It is possible to limit the analysis to those parts of the model most relevant to the particular situation. Therefore, the model can be perceived as a framework that provides an overview but the strategist does not necessarily have to perform all of the analyses every time. Aaker refers to the middle part – the *brand identity system* – as the heart of the model.

REFERENCES

Aaker, David (2002). *Building Strong Brands*. London: Simon & Schuster.
Hansen, Heidi (2016). *Branding. Teori, modeller, analyse,* 2nd edition. Frederiksberg: Samfundslitteratur.

THE CUSTOMER-BASED BRAND EQUITY MODEL (CBBE)

By Heidi Hansen

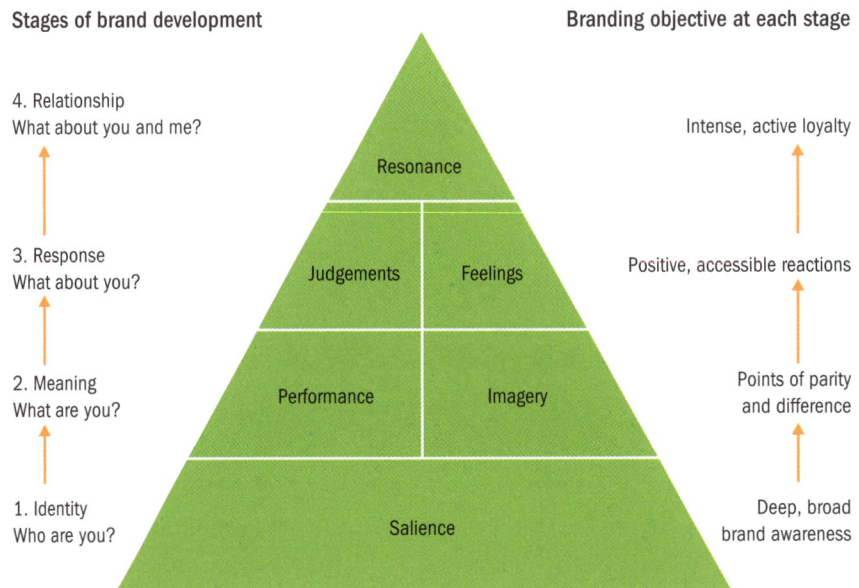

INTRODUCTION

The CBBE model considers how a strong brand is built by identifying a sequence of steps and a number of objectives that each need to be achieved successfully in order to move on in the brand building. The achievement of steps and objectives are contingent upon one another. As signaled by the name of the model – customer-based brand equity – successful branding relies on consumer perceptions.

WHAT IS THE MODEL ABOUT?

The CBBE model has been developed by Kevin Lane Keller, and the model is founded in the perception that the power of the brand lies in the minds of consumers. The CBBE model conceptualizes a brand as consisting of a number of building blocks divided into four steps represented in a pyramid. The pyramid illustrates a ladder, that is an ordering of the steps, thus signaling the sequence in which the steps ought to be accomplished. Each step addresses a fundamental question that customers invariably ask about brands, and in order to move up the ladder each subjacent step must be successfully accomplished. That is, meaning cannot be established unless identity has been created and so on. The left side of the pyramid represents USP (unique selling proposition) or the functional benefits of the brand whereas the right side of the pyramid represents ESP, that is the emotional benefits of the brand.

The first step in the pyramid is about establishing a unique brand identity that makes the brand stand out in the market. *Salience* thus relates to brand awareness that is expressed as how easily the brand is evoked or recalled, and the goal is to make the brand top-of-mind. The second step in the pyramid is *Performance* and *Imagery*, both of which are related to brand meaning. *Performance* addresses how a product or service attempts to meet functional needs and to what extent it satisfies these needs and wants. Key attributes of Performance are quality, design, product reliability, durability, and price. When a benchmark is performed, the brand ought to be evaluated against other brands in the same price range. *Performance* is thus about tangible product elements, whereas *Imagery* is about how people think about the brand abstractly. *Imagery* addresses the consumer's psychological or social needs, and important attributes of Imagery are purchase and usage situations, brand personality, values, history, and heritage. Imagery is about self-expressive benefits and plays a part in how the consumer is able to stage him-

or herself by use of the brand. Imagery may involve the use of celebrities in market communications or the use of symbolic personalities such as Ronald McDonald or the Michelin Man.

The third step in the pyramid is about brand response, which is what consumers think or feel about the brand. Responses may arise from the head – *Judgement* – or the heart – *Feelings*. Response is produced by brand meaning, i.e. Performance and Imagery. *Judgement* relates to the consumer's opinion and evaluation based on how the consumer puts together all the different associations resulting from Performance and Imagery. Judgement is based on evaluation of brand performance such as product benefits as well as how personally relevant consumers find the brand depending on whether the brand is viewed as appropriate and meaningful. *Feelings* relates to consumers' emotional response to the brand and a key attribute is how the brand affects the consumer's feelings about herself and her relationship with others or the brand. Keller (2003) identifies six feelings as important brand-building feelings: warmth, fun, excitement, security, social approval, and self-respect.

When the first five steps are successfully accomplished, it is possible to move on to the final step in the CBBE model, which is *Resonance*. Resonance focuses on the ultimate relationship and level of identification between the brand and the consumer. If consumer and brand are "in sync", the consumer experiences intense loyalty towards the brand, which results in repeat purchases and rejection of competing brands. Examples of brands that experience intense loyalty are Coca Cola and iPhone.

HOW CAN YOU USE THE MODEL?

The CBBE model is a tool for planning and analysis, and the model is able to guide a company when it comes to branding. The model can be used to structure branding activities by pointing out the six building blocks and ensure that all six blocks are given attention.

The model can also be used to gain an overview of the brand and evaluate the strength of each building block. It is important for a company to be aware of both strengths and weaknesses in order to address the right issues. Accordingly, a company ought to evaluate each building block regularly. Which blocks are standing strong? Which blocks need attention? The model can also form the basis of collection of quantitative or qualitative primary data, since the model can function as a frame of reference when questions are being worked out, and thus the CBBE model can ensure that the analyst remembers to cover all aspects.

WHAT ARE THE SHORTCOMINGS AND WEAKNESSES OF THE MODEL?

The model considers how a strong brand is built, but it is always possible to question the choice of building blocks as well as their sequence. A brand is a social construction; it is simply a collection of perceptions held in the mind of the consumer. Brand equity is thus intangible, and the CBBE model is just one way to conceptualize a brand.

REFERENCES

Hansen, Heidi (2016). *Branding. Teori, modeller, analyse*, 2nd edition. Frederiksberg: Samfundslitteratur.

Keller, Kevin L. (2003). *Strategic Brand Management: Building, Measuring, and Managing Brand Equity*. Upper Saddle River: Pearson/Prentice Hall.

BRAND ARCHITECTURE
By Heidi Hansen

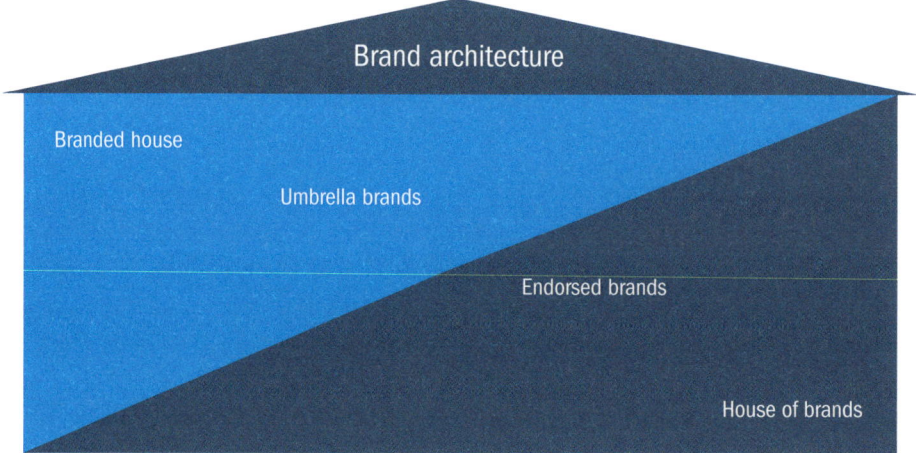

INTRODUCTION

The Brand Architecture illustrates how a company may use a number of different strategies in managing its brand portfolio. The *branded house strategy* represents one end of the spectrum. When a branded house strategy is applied, all products are branded as a corporate brand and thus all brand value is built around a single brand name. The exact opposite strategy is represented by the *house of brands strategy*, in which sub-brands are marketed as stand-alone brands that are branded individually.

WHAT IS THE MODEL ABOUT?

The Brand architecture illustrates the relationship between corporate brand and sub-brands by outlining four main strategies. In a *branded house strategy* (also known as corporate branding), the company employs a single (master) brand to span all of its offerings. Following this strategy, everything (the house) is branded as one single (corporate) brand, and accordingly all brand value is built around this single brand. The strength of this strategy is that all marketing activities can be concentrated to promote a single brand, allowing for more media exposure. The weakness of the strategy is a low degree of risk diversification since there is only one brand, and negative publicity will therefore affect all of the company's offerings.

The antipole to a branded house strategy is a *house of brands strategy,* which is also termed a one-product-one-brand strategy. Following this strategy, each sub-brand operates independently, and the corporate brand is invisible. An example of this strategy is Mars Inc., which markets the chocolate bar Mars as a corporate brand (branded house), while a great number of other brands are managed as a house of brands such as Dolmio, Uncle Ben's, Dove, Royal Canin, Whiskas, Hubba Bubba, and Skittles. Sub-brands that are branded as stand-alone brands will typically be perceived as independent corporate brands by consumers, and an advantage of this strategy is that sub-brands can be targeted a specific audience in order to create a top-of-mind brand in the category. The strategy also allows for flexibility in the brand portfolio, and sub-brands may be bought or sold without affecting other sub-brands. The downside of the strategy is that there is no synergy in the brand communication. It is thus a cost-intensive strategy given that every sub-brand must be nurtured independently. The pros and the cons of the two ends of the spectrum – branded house and house of brands – can be summarized as follows:

	PROS	CONS
Branded house	• Only one brand to nurture – synergy in brand communication • All resources are concentrated to promote a single brand – only one identity to manage • Simple communication – greater visibility • Easier to attract highly skilled employees (people prefer to work for well-reputed companies)	• All eggs in one basket – negative publicity may harm all offerings • The brand might be tightly associated to a certain product category (hindering portfolio development) • Risk of diluting the brand value (if the brand must embrace too many diverse products) • Lack of coherence in the brand portfolio – blurring of brand identity
House of brands	• Allows for a clear positioning to dominate niche segments • Risk diversification • Flexibility in composing the brand portfolio • Ability to sell sub-brands without affecting the rest of the brand portfolio	• The corporate brand is weak • No synergy in brand communication • High level of marketing costs – the more brands to promote, the higher the costs

Between these two ends of the spectrum, it is possible to combine the corporate brand and the sub-brands in a number of different ways, and thus choosing which of the above pros and cons to select or avoid. In the Brand Architecture, the relationship between corporate brand and sub-brand is illustrated by the light and dark blue colour. The light blue colour represents the corporate brand, and the dark blue colour represents the sub-brand.

In the left side of the model, the light blue colour dominates, thus signaling that the corporate brand is the main brand (or the only brand). In the branded house strategy, there is only one brand and all of the company (the house) is branded under this corporate brand name. A pure corporate brand strategy is rare as most companies need to differentiate their products in one way or another. One way to differentiate the sub-brands in a branded house strategy is to use a strategy of *graduation*. The graduation strategy combines the corporate brand name with a number or a letter to set the products apart as seen with the car manufacturer Citroen and their cars C1, C3, C4, and so on. Another way to differentiate the sub-brands in a branded house strategy is to use a strategy of *denomination*. The denomination strategy combines the corporate brand name with a generic product name such as Heinz Tomato Ketchup, Heinz BBQ Baked

Beans, Heinz Real Mayonnaise, Heinz Pickles & Relish, and so on. The essence of the branded house strategy is to concentrate all brand value in a single brand name, thus avoiding the introduction of new brand names that eventually could build an independent brand identity. Accordingly, products are being differentiated by using neutral designations such as number, letters or generic product labels. Sub-brands are represented by the dark blue colour in the Brand Architecture model, and the more space the dark blue colour takes up in the model, the more independently sub-brands are being branded.

The *umbrella strategy* is characterized by a symmetric relationship between corporate brand and sub-brand. The corporate brand functions as an overall umbrella – a platform that creates a joint frame of reference and functions as a driver for each sub-brand. The sub-brands, on the other hand, represent a unique identity that can be targeted different consumer segments.

When an *endorsed strategy* is applied, the corporate brand plays only a minor driver role. The corporate brand mainly serves as an endorser that can provide reassurance and credibility as seen for instance in the case of VW that endorses Skoda. In marketing material, the sub-brand will be at the center, and the corporate brand only serves as a sign of endorsement.

HOW CAN YOU USE THE MODEL?

The Brand Architecture model illustrates a spectrum of branding strategies with branded house at one end of the spectrum and house of brands at the opposite end. A company may apply more than one strategy, especially if there is a large portfolio of brands. There is no "best strategy" as each strategy provides a set of pros and cons. It is, therefore, important to weigh the pros and cons in order to compose the most optimal mix of strategies. Today's society is characterized by a lot of noise in the public sphere, which calls for a strategy of synergy in brand communication, but if some sub-brands target very different consumer segments or if they represent incompatible brand values that calls for a strategy of independency and separate brand identities.

The Brand Architecture can be used to map all of the company's brand and to take stock of the brand portfolio. It is important to consider whether the company applies the most optimal mix of strategies or if some brands could beneficially be moved towards a branded house or house of brands strategy based on the pros and cons represented by each strategy.

WHAT ARE THE SHORTCOMINGS AND WEAKNESSES OF THE MODEL?

The Brand Architecture only focuses on the relationship between corporate brand and sub-brand within the same company. Accordingly, the model does not include co-branding or celebrity branding, which represent cooperation between two or more companies.

The Brand Architecture is a conceptual model that provides an overview of pros and cons of different strategies and thereby assists companies in putting together the most optimal mix of strategies. However, in real life it will be possible to observe examples of branding strategies that fit neither of the strategies described in the model, seeing that the creativity of brand managers may surpass the rigidity of a model.

REFERENCES

Aaker, David A. & Erich Joachimstaler (2000). The Brand Relationship Spectrum: The Key to the Brand Architecture Challenge. *California Management Review*, 42 (4): 8-22.

Hansen, Heidi (2016). *Branding. Teori, modeller, analyse*, 2nd edition. Frederiksberg: Samfundslitteratur.

Kunde, Jesper (2001). *Unik nu… eller aldrig*. Copenhagen: Børsens Forlag.

DISTRIBUTION STRATEGY (PLACE)

By Kim Buch-Madsen

Distribution Strategy

Channel management
1. Screening and dealer choice
2. Motivation of dealers
3. Evaluation and control
4. Collaboration and conflict management

Channel strategy
1. Design of distribution channels
2. Market coverage
3. Channel integration

INTRODUCTION

The model provides an overview and map of the most important elements of a distribution strategy. It demonstrates what strategic decisions should be made and what management tasks should be solved in the Place parameter in the marketing mix (see 8 P model, page 56).

WHAT IS THE MODEL ABOUT?

Distribution strategy is divided into two parts: *channel strategy* and *channel management*. Both take into account the company, product, market, and competition that constitute the context of channel strategy and channel management.

Channel strategy is about the design of distribution channel(s), choice of market coverage, and integration between individual parts of the chain.

Design of distribution channel(s): The starting point for a distribution strategy is to determine how many and which links the company will use to reach the customers. Is there a need for intermediaries, or can/will the company sell directly to end customers? If there are intermediaries, is there a need for a wholesaler, or can you sell directly to large retail chains? Should the product be sold fully or partially online? If so, should it supplement or replace retail stores? These decisions depend upon a wide range of market conditions, the product, the competition and the company, such as: Are customers widely and geographically dispersed or are there fewer and more concentrated? Are there special requirements for technical expertise or service that dealers should honor? Do customers have specific expectations as to where they usually purchase products or in which product categories the company's product should be included?

Market coverage: Through *intensive distribution*, the goal is to seek as many dealers as possible and as wide of coverage as possible. This is common for goods that are often purchased and customers are reluctant to travel far to obtain. An example is FMCG (fast moving consumer goods) as found in supermarkets. *Exclusive distribution* is often used for focused or niche strategies, and dealers are hand-picked. *Selective distribution* is an intermediate solution to increase expansion, but at the same time, is considerably more selective than *intensive distribu-*

tion. It is more important that the product is available in the right places than being available in as many places as possible.

Integration: This deals with how closely the individual parts of the distribution channel are linked. *Conventional channels* are collaborations between parts, which are independent companies, and the counterpole is *vertical integration* where the manufacturer owns its dealers. *Franchising* is the middle road, where you seek to combine the benefits of both opposing poles. Local franchisees are independent businesses, but within the framework of a central franchisor, which offers access to, for example, the brand, joint marketing, education, purchasing systems, etc., and in return the franchisee pays a fee for these benefits.

Channel management is about dealer choice, motivation, evaluation, cooperation, and conflict management.

Screening and selection of retailers: Once the strategy is in place, the next step is to assess and select the most attractive dealers. For example, if a selective coverage strategy is chosen for a piece of furniture, should it be negotiated through a homeware, furniture, budget or office supply store or online or through an exclusive specialty store? And if a furniture store is chosen, which chain would be the best?

Motivation: Just because the product is part of a dealer's assortment, does not guarantee active sales efforts. Incentives must be created, so dealers actively expose and sell the product in the store, via the website, in daily customer contact, and in retailers' market communications online and offline. Among the tools to motivate the dealers are profit margins, discounts, delivery terms, bonuses, product information, service, and marketing support.

Evaluation and control: The manufacturer continually assesses whether the dealers perform according to agreements and goals and whether they remain the best choice in relation to other options. Compliance with agreements and rules of play are also subject to evaluation, for example in relation to what competing products the dealer sells and under what conditions.

Collaboration and conflict management: Manufacturers and dealers are both collaborators and competitors with both common and conflicting interests. Therefore, negotiating strength is a core factor, as illustrated by Porter's Five Forces model. Under these working conditions, there will always be the risk of conflict related to the good cooperation that is and should be the norm. It is, thus, a key task of distribution management to nurse the relationship, prevent conflicts, and solve them when they arise. Clear agreements, and if necessary, contracts, can prevent conflicts from occurring.

HOW CAN YOU USE THE MODEL?

The model gives an overall understanding of which strategic choices are to be made and which key tasks are to be solved within the Place parameter in the marketing mix (8 P).

The model can be used to describe and analyze a reseller system, whether you are a manufacturer or dealer, and whether it is your own or the competitor's reseller system. The model can also be used as a rough working plan to design a dealer system from the beginning.

Finally, the model can function as a checklist, outlining key areas that must be managed and in sync with one another for the Place parameter in the marketing mix to be most effective. Thereby the model can also be a rough diagnostic tool for initial assessments of why a negotiation system works or not.

WHAT ARE THE SHORTCOMINGS AND WEAKNESSES OF THE MODEL?

First and foremost, it is a strategically-oriented model that demonstrates which key tasks are to be solved within the Place parameter, but it does not provide guidelines as to how to resolve them.

In addition, the model only takes partly into account the fact that the Place parameter is part of the overall marketing mix of the 8 Ps, which needs to function as a whole and reinforce each other. The model generally examines the Place parameter isolated from the other parameters: Price, Promotion, People, etc.

The model takes into account that the parties in a distribution chain both have common and conflicting interests but does not describe where and how. It does not clarify the specific tasks for which the distribution chain is responsible. One of those being logistics, which is of great importance as to whether the system can move the goods quickly and efficiently to customers with the least possible costs. This applies, for example, to transport, warehousing, purchasing and transport planning, order processing, exchange/return options, IT systems, etc.

Finally, the model depends on an implicit assumption that it is the manufacturer who selects its dealers. It may as well be reversed and depend on the parties' mutual bargaining power and the intensity of competition. Often, in practice, it is not a question of which dealers the manufacturer desires but as to which dealers the manufacturer can access.

REFERENCES

Andersen, Finn Rolighed, Bjarne Warming Jensen, Mette Risgaard Olsen et al. (2015). *International markedsføring*, 5th edition. Copenhagen: Trojka.

Buch-Madsen, Kim (2005). *Marketing – klart og koncentreret*. Frederiksberg: Samfundslitteratur.

Dent, Julian & Michael White (2018). *Sales and Marketing Channels: How to Build and Manage Distribution Strategy*, 3rd edition. London: Kogan Page Limited.

Jobber, David & Fiona Ellis-Chadwick (2016). *Principles and Practice of Marketing*, 8th edition. Maidenhead: McGraw-Hill Education.

3. MARKET COMMUNICATION AND SALES

TIBBLE'S PLANNING CYCLE
By Sine Nørholm Just

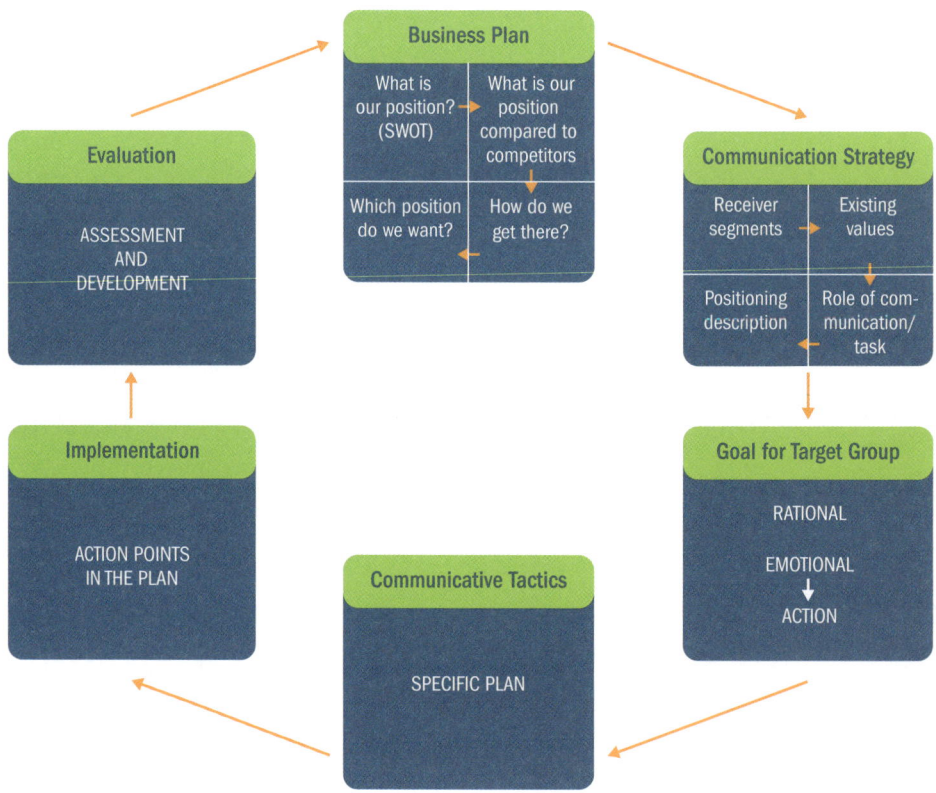

INTRODUCTION

The model demonstrates how specific communication campaigns can be linked to an organization's communication strategy and its overall business plan. The planning cycle assumes there is no linear relationship between general strategy and specific communication, but rather a circular process where what you learn through the specific communication process, can be used in further strategic work.

WHAT IS THE MODEL ABOUT?

The model is basically about communication planning – and the link between the concrete plan and the overall strategy. One of Tibble's main points is that many companies use the strategy concept too diffusely, and thereby, incorrectly. To remedy this, the model demonstrates what strategic communication is and how it can be planned and implemented.

The planning cycle moves through six steps from an overall level to an actual level – and back again. Each of the six steps consists of several elements:

Step 1 is the development phase of the business plan, which entails the overall strategy. Here, an analysis of the organization's current position must first be made, focusing on the organization itself and its relation to its environment. This can be performed with tools such as SWOT and PESTEL. Based on this, the goal is set for the organization, and the overall plan of how to achieve the goal is defined. The organization thereby attains its rationale, that is, its strategy, which can then be made concrete in relation to communication efforts.

Step 2 is to establish a communication strategy that should not only be based upon the organization itself but also includes segmentation of the possible target groups and a study of the link between the different target groups' existing perception of the organization's values and the desired position. On this foundation, the role of communication can be determined. Does it, for example, need to reinforce an existing relationship between the organization and its target group(s)? Should new relationships be built? Once arranged, one can develop a message that will penetrate the entire communication.

Step 3, considers how the set goals are related to the target group. The final goal will usually be a form of action, but rational and emotional relationships need to be built in order to achieve the goals.

Step 4 is the preparation of communicative tactics, i.e., the specific plan for communication efforts or the campaign, including the selection of specific media, genres, etc.

The plan is carried out in step 5, and at step 6 implementation is evaluated. This final step goes back to the beginning because the study of implemented communication should be part of the development of new strategic goals. Experience from previous communication can be used to inform future strategic communication.

HOW CAN YOU USE THE MODEL?

The model can be utilized as a guideline as to what tasks are included in strategic communication processes. It has tremendous strength in linking overall strategy and specific campaigns and can be used to ensure coherence between strategic and tactical levels. In addition, using the model can ensure that the overall strategy is continually informed by the experience gained during the process. It is a good tool for planning strategic communication.

WHAT ARE THE SHORTCOMINGS AND WEAKNESSES OF THE MODEL?

In the presentation of the planning cycle, Tibble focuses on explaining what is meant by strategy and how an organization's overall strategy should inform the communication strategy. This neglects the question as to how to specifically plan and implement a communication campaign, and the model must be supplemented with other tools. Similarly, a business plan cannot be developed based upon the planning cycle alone, as indicated directly in the model through the reference to the SWOT analysis. The model presents an overall framework for the planning cycle, which needs to be specified further at each step.

The model also has a significant weakness. It describes planning as a cyclical process, but suggest a step-by-step movement, moving completely around the cycle and not moving back and forth along the way. This is particularly problematic in the shift from steps 4 to 5, from planning to implementing communication. It does not take into account the dynamics that in reality impact the process. There is no room for continuous action and improvisation along the way.

Generally, the model provides a somewhat simplified picture as to how strategic communication actually takes place. There is too much faith in planning and too little focus on process. The great strength of the model is that it connects strategy and communication closely together. Its major weakness is that this link primarily goes from strategy to communication and gives the impression that communication can actually be planned. The model describes strategic communication as a more organized and controlled process than what is actually the case.

REFERENCES

Gulbrandsen, Ib Tunby & Sine Nørholm Just (2016). *Strategizing Communication. Theory and Practice*. Frederiksberg: Samfundslitteratur.

Tibble, Steve (1997). Developing communications strategy. *Journal of Communication Management*, 1 (4): 356-361.

THE COMMUNICATION PROCESS
By Kim Skjoldborg

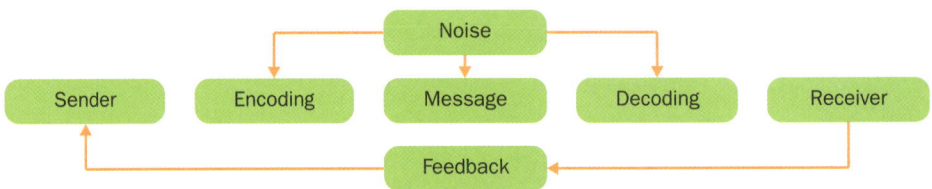

INTRODUCTION

The model describes the communication process between the sender and the receiver, and the steps to be accomplished for communication efforts to succeed, as well as the noise that may occur and interfere with the communication.

WHAT IS THE MODEL ABOUT?

This communication model is often credited to Schramm (1955). The model has formed the basis for several of the models that have since been created. It is a linear communication model where the sender wishes to convey a message to one or more recipients. Occasionally, the model is referred to as the "needle model." This is due to the basic idea of the model of a one to one transmission of the message from the sender to the receiver.

The starting point is a sender who wishes to convey a message to a recipient. The sender is typically a company or brand. The company or brand will be the sender, but the task of designing the communication strategy can be placed with an external advertising agency. Initially, a company may have different communication goals. For example, it may be to increase awareness of or change the recipient's attitude towards the company.

The next step in the model is the coding of the message. The sender must consider how the message is best transmitted to the recipient. In fact, a message can be conveyed in a multitude of ways. The considerations remain the same whether it is a presentation for a small group internally in the company, a sales presentation to a customer or a nationwide advertising campaign. Regardless of the size of the target group, the sender must consider which combination of text, images, and audio is most effective in communicating the message. The composition of the message is the main factor that has the most effect on communication.

The third phase of the model is the message. The phase covers how the message is to be conveyed. The sender must decide which in channels the message is to be communicated. The company can choose from many different media: print, TV, radio, online, direct mail, outdoor, mobile or other. The sender must consider how effective the media is in reaching the target group, what is the cost and whether they can communicate the message.

The fourth phase is the decoding of the message. The recipient is exposed to the message and decodes it. It is very important that the recipient decodes the message as the sender wishes. The decoding of the message depends upon who the recipient is. 360 million people have watched the video "FourFiveSeconds" with Rihanna, Kanye West, and Paul McCartney. The younger section of the target group will surely perceive Rihanna and Kanye West as good people who help an old guitarist kickstart his career, while others may perceive that Sir Paul McCartney assists in putting two young artists in the spotlight. It is the same video, but it can be interpreted differently depending on who is the recipient. Interpretation depends upon the recipient's knowledge and experience. It is important to remember that the recipient is selective in both the choice of messages they process and how they decode them.

The last two elements of the model are noise and feedback. "Noise" originally meant noise on the telephone line, but today noise is perceived as the factors that can adversely affect the process. For example, the message is competing with other advertisements on the website so that the recipient gets distracted during conveying the message. Feedback covers the response of the recipient.

HOW CAN YOU USE THE MODEL?

The model can be used to plan and implement different forms of communication. The model is typically used to plan an advertising campaign for a company or brand, but it can also be used in conjunction with a presentation to a person or small group of recipients. The considerations to be made and the phases that are undergone are essentially the same.

The communication model's strength is that it gives a good overview of the phases that are passed from sender to receiver. The model is simple and easy to understand. By thinking through the different phases and paying attention to them, the likelihood of efficient communication is increased.

The communication model can be used with the DAGMAR model. DAGMAR is used to clarify the objective of communication, while the communication model focuses on the steps to be taken to reach the goal.

WHAT ARE THE SHORTCOMINGS AND WEAKNESSES OF THE MODEL?

All models have a number of strengths and weaknesses, and that also applies to the communication model. The model clearly describes the phases of the communication process, but it gives no indication as to what to say and where in order to achieve the desired effect. Which message works best in the given situation and which combination of media will be most effective? The model provides no instructions for this.

Another weakness of the model is it assumes that the sender is active and the recipient is passive. But in many cases, the process begins with the receiver, who has a problem. Subsequently, the recipient actively searches for information, i.e., on the internet, which can help solve the problem. The process begins most often with a recipient who is actively seeking information.

The model does not take into account that most recipients are selective in their processing of market communication. The recipient is selective in all phases and most often choose what they will be exposed to, if they are attentive and how they choose to interpret the message. The consequence is that far fewer end up receiving the message than what the sender believes. The recipient screens and subsequently ignores messages due to lack of need or interest. The manner in which the message is interpreted is also selective. There is no guarantee that the recipient decodes the message as the sender desires.

Formally, it is a linear process where the recipient is placed at the end of the line. In fact, the recipient is already involved in the coding of the message. It's difficult to consider how to convey the message without having a clear picture of who is addressed.

In conclusion, it should be mentioned that the model does not take into account the fact that the recipient of the communication can convey further the message. It can be via "word of mouth" or social media. This is a positive effect as the message can be spread further and at a low cost. An alternative would be that the recipient is exposed to the message several times. The model, therefore, does not portray complete reality.

REFERENCES

Andersen, Finn Rolighed, Bjarne Warming Jensen, Mette Risgaard Olsen et al. (2015). *International markedsføring*, 5th edition. Copenhagen: Trojka.

Belch, George E. & Michael A. Belch (2015). *Advertising and Promotion*, 10th edition. Montreal: Chenelière McGraw-Hill.

Egan, John (2015). *Marketing Communications*, 2nd edition. Los Angeles: Sage Publications.

Jobber, David & Fiona Ellis-Chadwick (2016). *Principles and Practice of Marketing*, 8th edition. Maidenhead: McGraw-Hill Education.

PAID, OWNED AND EARNED MEDIA MODEL
By Christian Grandjean

MEDIA TYPE	PAID MEDIA	OWNED MEDIA	EARNED MEDIA
Definition	The company buys access to placement in certain media and control over messages and timing	The company's own media	Media on which the company earns the right to communicate
Examples	TV, commercials, ads	A company's: Website, direct mail, own social media, newsletters	Press reviews, blog reviews Word-of-Mouth (WOM)
Benefits	Control of message and timing, wide coverage, measurable	Control of message and timing, cost-effective, measurable	High degree of credibility, cost-effective, partially measurable
Disadvantages	Noise Low credibility	Lower credibility Hard to reach the target audience	No control over message and timing; may be negative

INTRODUCTION

With the Paid, Owned and Earned Media Model, companies compose a media plan with types of media in which the company controls the messaging and types of media in which the company must earn the target audience's willingness to convey the company's messaging. This last media type is often seen as the most credible by customers but is also most difficult for the company to control.

WHAT IS THE MODEL ABOUT?

When a company is outlining a media plan in connection with a campaign, for example, it is important to include all relevant media types in the plan. Otherwise, the message may not reach all target groups. An effective media plan should typically contain both traditional push media and dialogue-oriented social media. To ensure the most efficient mix of channels, it is important to understand the strengths and weaknesses of the different media types. The Paid, Owned and Earned Media Model describes these differences.

HOW CAN YOU USE THE MODEL?

The Paid, Owned and Earned Media Model operates with three types of media. The individual media types depend on how much control the company has with the media and the message. The model demonstrates that individual media types cannot exist alone, but fulfill different purposes that influence and support each other.

It is therefore important to consider all media types for a media plan, so the different media complement one another. This ensures optimum media pressure and maximum impact.

Paid Media: Typical mass media with sender-defined messages. In these media a company has control over the message and timing. Paid media is typically utilized to create awareness and garner attention to a business or campaign. Examples of paid media are TV commercials, print and banner ads, radio advertising, and search engine advertising.

One of the challenges of this kind of media is the consumer does not seek this communication themselves, and therefore, may find the interruption as unwelcome or inappropriate or the content irrelevant.

Owned Media: In a company's own media, it has full control over the message and timing. Owned media is typically used to support image-creating efforts, campaigns, and sales because it is possible to thoroughly communicate nuanced information in the company's own channels, and it is cost-effective to produce and distribute. Examples of owned media are a company's own website, newsletters, own channels on social media, magazines, and events.

A primary challenge with this media type is it can be difficult to reach customers in the company's own media, target groups are aware of the company's commercial interests and the messaging is often seen as less credible.

Earned Media: The publicity that the company earns. It can include media whereby customers share their buying or user experiences, and it is the user who has control. The dialogue is visible to other customers, and the company and its products can, therefore, be mentioned numerous times in different channels.

The starting point for communication in earned media is often referred to as content. Its content is based on customers' interests (and not a typical advertising message from the company). The goal is for customers to capture and share the content as much as possible without the company having to pay for it. Examples of earned media are press coverage, blog reviews, and word-of-mouth communication. The disadvantage of this media type is the company has no control over what is communicated and when. In other words, the company gets the publicity that customers believe it deserves – good or bad. In earned media, only a customer's *experienced truth* counts, whether they are right or wrong.

WHAT ARE THE SHORTCOMINGS AND WEAKNESSES OF THE MODEL?

The Paid, Owned and Earned Media Model primarily provides an overview of the types of media, but it cannot be used to prepare a detailed media plan.

The model does not demonstrate that there is also an overlap between the different media types. Therefore, it is important to consider how different media types can be used for a planned effort. Examples of overlapping include the following scenarios:

- Although the model describes the difficulty in reaching a particular customer group through owned media, a campaign may garner enough interest that

customers themselves, will search for more information on the company's own channels. In this case, the owned media must be included in the plan.
- A company can post messages on its Facebook page, which according to the model is owned media. However, if the company's posts incite customer interest and the customers share the posts and their own comments, the page takes on the character of earned media. In this case, it is important to consider the features of both media types in the media plan.
- A company can purchase ad space on social media, such as Facebook. According to the model, this is paid media. At the same time, the company can post messages on its Facebook page, i.e., as an owned media type. Again, it is important to think of the features of both media types in the media plan.

REFERENCES

Andersen, Finn Rolighed, Bjarne Warming Jensen, Mette Risgaard Olsen et al. (2015). *International markedsføring*, 5th edition. Copenhagen: Trojka.

Andersen, Ole E., Svend Hollensen, Poul K. Faarup et al. (2016). *Moderne markedsføring*, 2nd edition. Copenhagen: Hans Reitzels Forlag.

Savar, Avi (2013). *Content to Commerce, Engaging Consumers Across Paid, Owned and Earned Channels*. New Jersey: John Wiley & Sons.

AIDA
By Ole E. Andersen

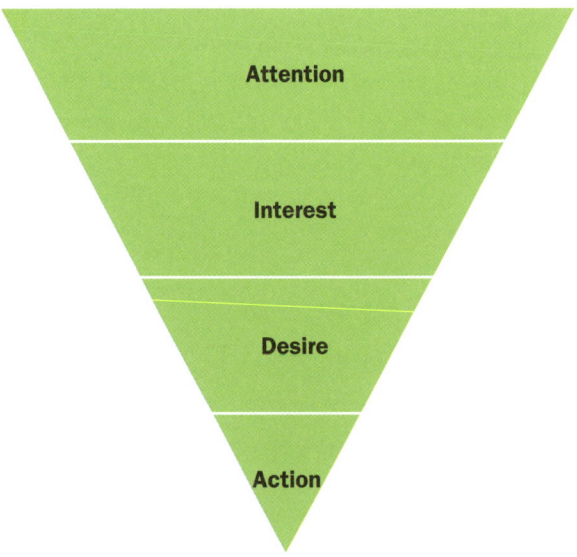

INTRODUCTION

The model shows at both the individual level and overall target group level the different phases of a customer's response to or receipt of promotional stimuli (in an effect hierarchy). The phases include Attention, Interest, Desire, and Action (AIDA).

WHAT IS THE MODEL ABOUT?

The model is a so-called "effect hierarchy model," dating all the way back to 1898 and is one of the oldest marketing models still in use. It illustrates the effect of a communication effort – whether it's offline or online, no matter where or how the target audience will be exposed on their customer journey as a result of the campaign: As a result of the communication effort, some people are aware of the message/brand (attention), fewer display interest in the brand, even fewer have the intention of buying, and finally, the fewest perform the desired action, whether it is the purchase of a branded product, a visit to a store or a change in behavior.

It is essentially a micro model (at the individual level), but it can also be considered a macro model, i.e., a model for the expected response to a promotional effort towards a given *target group*. AIDA *is not* a model for individual decision making.

The model is, of course, only giving theoretic guidelines for the general process from drawing attention to generating action. The nature of a campaign will depend on the purpose. On one side of the spectrum, a successful campaign can be an extensive awareness-raising campaign with relatively few final buyers or, on the other, a very narrow conversion campaign with relatively many buyers, among those who are aware of the brand. Levels of performance in each of the four phases will vary in a specific campaign depending, for example, on the product category, target group, competitive promotional activities, the scope of the campaign, creative strategy and selection of media.

HOW CAN YOU USE THE MODEL?

In addition to gaining knowledge of how communication works, the model can be used in two ways for planning promotional activities. First, it creates inspiration and structure to set quantitative goals at the different levels. How many of the target group are expected to be aware of a brand, and what percentage are expected to show a positive interest in the brand, etc.?

The objectives are set as percentages on each level, so a final expected number of buyers/actions can be estimated. The example below shows in each of the four phases the percentage of the entire target group for the campaign. Example:

PHASE	ATTENTION	INTEREST	DESIRE	ACTION
Objective as a percentage of target group	60 %	35 %	18 %	8 %
Objective as a percentage of previous stage	60 %	58 % (of 60 %)	51 % (of 58 %)	44 % (of 51 %)

The objectives and calculations can also be arranged so that the numbers in each stage are a percentage of the previous stage, after which the percentages are to be multiplied to obtain the expected sales/result (second row).

The percentage of action compared to the target group is 60 % x 58 % x 51 % x 44 % = 8 %. The two methods for setting goals are both good and lead to the same result.

You can also use the model as a checklist when compiling and analyzing different types of promotional material, such as online and offline ads and direct mail. The model raises several questions like "Are there (enough) awareness-creating items?" or "Does the ad create interest and reasons for purchase intentions and is it giving the receiver a call to action through a "click here" to visit a website or Facebook page, call a phone number, etc.?"

WHAT ARE THE SHORTCOMINGS AND WEAKNESSES OF THE MODEL?

The model has two weaknesses in its primary form of use, that is, setting goals:

1. It lacks certain levels/phases in the recipients' possible responses.
2. It is not specific enough to set concrete measurements.

Taking a look at the first weakness, the AIDA model lacks an important phase between Attention and Interest, namely brand perception or association, i.e., a decidedly cognitive phase that goes deeper than just Awareness/Attention. One can also argue that, after the Action phase, there should be an S for Satisfaction. It must be a value-creating or need-satisfying action (Action) that causes the buyer to repeat his behavior.

The second weakness, the model's lack of precision, can be exemplified at the first level, Attention. Attention, we usually measure by knowledge. But is it unaided or aided recall and knowledge of what? Similarly, Interest and Desire must be specified into, for example, attitudes, preferences, which brands will you consider, and an operational measurement of purchase intentions.

REFERENCES

De Pelsmacker, Patrick, Maggie Geuens & Joeri Van den Bergh (2013). *Marketing Communications: A European Perspective*. 5th edition. Harlow: Pearson Education Limited.

Kotler, Philip T., Kevin Lane Keller, Mairead Brady et al. (2016). *Marketing Management*. 3rd edition. Harlow: Pearson Education Limited.

DAGMAR
By Sine Nørholm Just

- Category need
- Brand awareness
- Brand knowledge/comprehension
- Brand attitude
- Brand purchase intention
- Purchase facilitation
- Purchase
- Satisfaction
- Brand loyalty

INTRODUCTION

DAGMAR is an abbreviation for Defining Advertising Goals for Measured Advertising Results and is a tool that assists in systematically setting goals for advertising campaigns and other forms of market communication. The overall purpose of the model is to set relevant and definite goals for the specific campaign and to ensure it can subsequently be measured if the objectives have been achieved.

WHAT IS THE MODEL ABOUT?

DAGMAR is a so-called effect hierarchy model, which means it is based on the assumption that the target group goes through different phases in its response to market communication, from attention to interest to desire and action (Attention, Interest, Desire, Action; see AIDA model, page 116). DAGMAR presents a more detailed set of possible goals and outcomes as a result of communication efforts, as opposed to other effect hierarchies.

First, there are a number of goals that focus on creating awareness. The "Category need" is about the target group's basic awareness of the product category and experienced need for this category. Such a need is a prerequisite for promoting a specific brand. "Brand awareness" is about the target group's awareness of the brand. Given the target group has experienced a need for the product, does the target group know the specific brand to meet that need? Brand knowledge/comprehension and brand attitude build on the target group's awareness of the brand. What do members of the target group know about the brand, do they understand it, and what is their attitude towards it?

The next set of goals goes from attention, knowledge, and attitude to action. "Brand purchase intention" focuses on the target group's desire to purchase products from the brand, while "purchase facilitation" highlights how easy it is for the target audience to fulfill this desire. The purchase is the actual intention of buying.

Last, there are a set of goals that concentrate on the target group's experience and opinion after purchases are made. "Satisfaction" is the customer's happiness with the brand, while "brand loyalty" deals with the target group's loyalty. How many customers will purchase the product again and how often? Will (part of) the target group recommend the product and/or otherwise speak positively about the brand?

HOW CAN YOU USE THE MODEL?

The DAGMAR model can be used in three different but ideally coherent ways. Firstly, it can be used to analyze the target group's relation to the brand before the communication effort. This allows you to get a concrete idea on which aspect the communication should be focused. For example, if a new and innovative product is introduced, a recognized need among the target group would need to be created and thereby, a market for the product. Only thereafter it is relevant to promote the specific brand or a call for purchase. Vice-versa, if it is a well-known brand with a strong market position, the focus may be on getting even more buyers. And if all relevant target groups are already saturated, customer satisfaction and loyalty would the most appropriate goals.

Secondly, you can set specific goals for each of the areas you have chosen to focus on in your communication efforts. For example, if the target is to achieve increased brand recognition, the specific goal may be that 90 % of the target group should be able to recall the brand, or if the focus is on increasing purchases, the target may be 20 % additional sales, etc.

Thirdly, setting specific goals and objectives provide an opportunity to concretely measure success. Did the communication efforts meet the established goals??

WHAT ARE THE SHORTCOMINGS AND WEAKNESSES OF THE MODEL?

DAGMAR's strength lies in establishing relevant goals as a basis for measuring results, while also reducing the complexity of the communication process. The model requires a clear before and after, between which the communication unfolds as a linear transfer from sender to receiver based on the premise that success can be measured as a direct effect of communication. It is rarely that simple in practice. On the contrary, communication is usually a widely complicated process with many different and often indirect effects. It is incorrect to assume goals will be achieved simply because they are clear and well-defined. It is also uncertain if clear and well-defined goals can be measured. In other words, if too much focus is put on predefined goals, it may lead to lack of insight as to what the communication actually achieves.

In the same manner, the model's hierarchical thinking creates a good starting point for identifying the target group's relationship with the brand, but it does not take into consideration that people's decision-making processes do not always follow the order of elements that the model lists. People may, for example, purchase a product without knowledge of or sympathy for the brand or vice versa they can know and sympathize with a brand without actually buying its product(s). This makes it possible for the analysis to be misleading, even if it is correct.

Together, these two criticisms mean that one cannot always determine goals precisely and accurately, and it is not as simple to achieve these goals as the DAGMAR model leads to believe. DAGMAR sets a solid framework for communication but does not describe how the communication actually takes place in the context of setting goals and measuring results.

REFERENCES

Andersen, Finn Rolighed, Bjarne Warming Jensen, Mette Risgaard Olsen et al. (2015). *International markedsføring*, 5th edition. Copenhagen: Trojka.

Andersen, Ole E., Svend Hollensen, Poul K. Faarup et al. (2016). *Moderne markedsføring*, 2nd edition. Copenhagen: Hans Reitzels Forlag.

Colley, Russell H. (1961). *Defining Advertising Goals for Measured Advertising Results*. New York: Association of National Advertisers.

De Pelsmacker, Patrick, Maggie Geuens & Joeri Van den Bergh (2013). *Marketing Communications: A European Perspective*. 5th edition. Harlow: Pearson.

EFFECTIVE FREQUENCY (IN MEDIA PLANNING)
By Ole E. Andersen

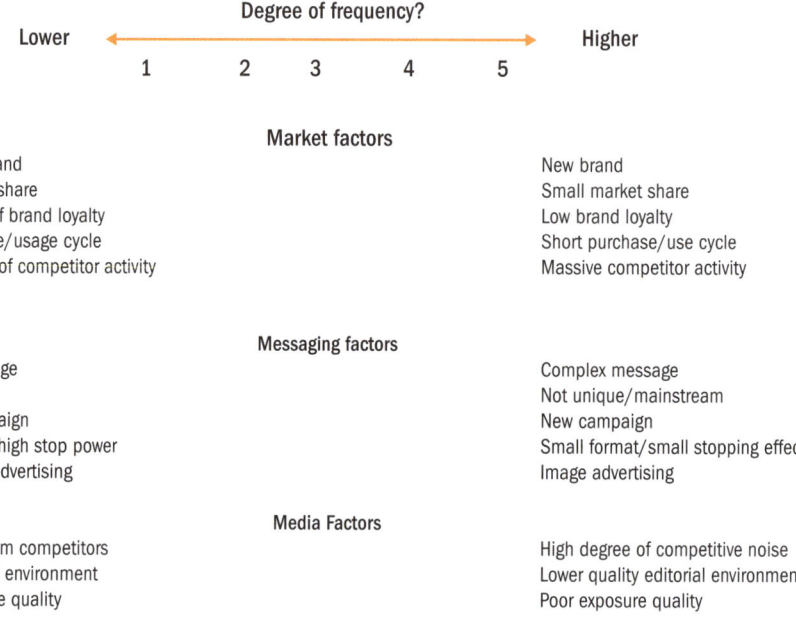

INTRODUCTION

When considering the media pressure of an advertising campaign, the model demonstrates the factors relevant to estimating the number of times a person in the target group should be exposed to a campaign in order to achieve its desired effect.

WHAT IS THE MODEL ABOUT?

We are in media planning, i.e., the phase in marketing planning where the media must be chosen for the advertising campaign for the target group to see the campaign, and also the number of times the advertisements need to be placed, so the recipients are exposed to the campaign sufficient number of times. Using commonly used terms in the industry you would say media pressure must secure exposures in the target group in terms of both "net coverage" (reach) in the target group and "frequency" (the number of times the recipients are exposed). It is a known fact that one exposure is rarely enough.

In this regard, an important question is *how many times a campaign should be seen by a person in the target group* to achieve the desired effect. This is called the determination of the effective frequency or rather a pre-estimation of the effective frequency on a systematic basis. It is important both for media plan costs and to avoid underexposing the target group (so the campaign does not work) and overexposing (wasting money and even risk of annoying consumers).

HOW CAN YOU USE THE MODEL?

The model contains four types of factors with 14 specific variables that should be included in the effective frequency estimate of a specific campaign, namely market conditions, message, media, and target group factors. The model is a "questionnaire" to be completed for the campaign and the market situation. There is no definite answer as to what is the right frequency. Each campaign is unique. A typical starting point for an average campaign is a frequency of three, and for a specific campaign, there are conditions that draw up and down from the average situation.

The practical application is that, prior to the campaign, the marketer evaluates each of the 14 variables on a five-point scale that corresponds to the number of exposures. For example, in a campaign for a highly established brand with a fairly large market share, one respectively two exposures, are registered. Both indicate a lower frequency than if it was a campaign for a new brand with a small market share.

The process produces an estimated average of effective frequency, e.g., 3.7, which is obtained as the sum of the responses to the 14 variables divided by 14. Since it is an average with a certain spread, it is in practice "translated" to a *frequency range* of between two and six exposures. It is within this range that the campaign is assumed to have an optimal effect. The scale *per variable* is no higher than five, but in a world with a lot of advertising noise, the upper interval point must often be higher than five. Many media agencies have a frequency model in their software programs based on experiences from previous campaigns they have assisted in planning and implementing.

WHAT ARE THE SHORTCOMINGS AND WEAKNESSES OF THE MODEL?

One defect in the model is that there is *no weighting* of the 14 variables. There may be a difference between the importance of the brand having a large market share or expecting little competition. It is also a weakness that some variables will be based on completely *subjective* assessments, such as the extent to which the campaign is unique and the extent to which the target group is accessible.

It can also be discussed as to whether the 14 variables reflect all relevant factors important to the effective frequency. Is there a difference between a campaign for cars and one for flights, even though both product categories are characterized by "long purchase cycles?" Is it important that a campaign has several different creative variants with the same main message? These questions can be answered by supplementing the quantitative model with qualitative assessments of each campaign.

Finally, an academic objection can be made that the frequency issue stems from the classic theory of advertising as a strong influence on consumers. This assumption is increasingly challenged by empiricism on advertising fatigue, "banner blindness," and lack of confidence in advertisers' messages.

REFERENCES

Andersen, Ole E., Svend Hollensen, Poul K. Faarup et al. (2016). *Moderne Markedsføring*, 2nd edition. Copenhagen: Hans Reitzels Forlag.

De Pelsmacker, Patrick, Maggie Geuens & Joeri Van den Bergh (2018). *Marketing Communications: A European Perspective,* 6th edition. Harlow: Pearson Education Limited.

Fill, Chris & Sarah Turnbull (2016). *Marketing Communications*, 7th edition. Harlow: Pearson Education Limited.

Sepstrup, Preben & Pernille Fruensgaard Øe (2010). *Tilrettelæggelse af information – kommunikations- og kampagneplanlægning*, 4th edition. Copenhagen: Academica.

THE SALES PROCESS
By Kim Buch-Madsen

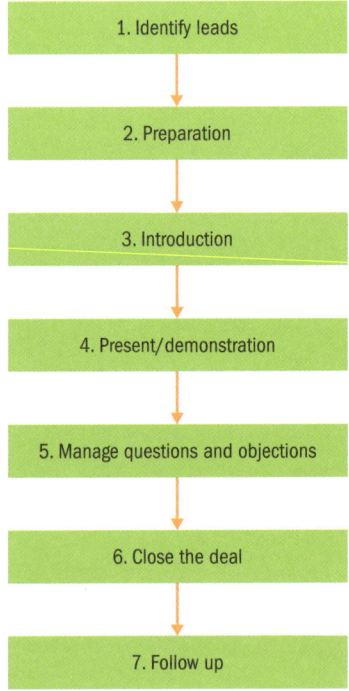

INTRODUCTION

The model describes what phases an effective sales meeting goes through, what is taking place in each phase of the meeting between the seller and the customer, and what are the seller's tasks in each phase.

WHAT IS THE MODEL ABOUT?

The course and the most important activities in the individual phases are:

1. **Identify leads:** Find people or companies with a need for the product. This is accomplished, for example, through internet research, in business media, professional networks, collaborators, fairs and seminars, and last but not least, canvassing (unannounced contact to customers, typically by telephone).
2. **Preparation:** Obtain maximum knowledge about the company and the person or persons to meet, schedule a meeting, prepare or select relevant sales material, samples or product demonstrations.
3. **Introduction:** The first task is to capture the customer's positive attention and create a positive atmosphere. The first few minutes of contact between people is crucial. The seller's goal is to signal professionalism, sympathy, dedication, and credibility. Communication is crucial, and it is about much more than what we say. Over 90 % of the impression the counterpart receives stems from nonverbal communication such as body language, mimic, voice, handshake, and attire.
4. **Present/demonstrate:** "What's in it for me?" is every customer's attitude. The customer focuses on what problems or needs the product can solve. Often product characteristics are only interesting because of what they can do for the customer. The customer thinks holistic in the "whole package" including the delivery system and the company that will deliver the product. This phase is not only about creating a trust in the product, but also in the company's processes and qualities as a business partner.
5. **Manage questions and objections:** If the customer is interested, negotiation begins with questions, objections, and requirements. These can range from "It's too expensive, can you offer a better price?" to "Can you deliver faster?" or "There is no money in the budget before next year" to "We are pleased with our current supplier, so you have to offer something special." The salesperson

must anticipate these objections and questions, be prepared to respond to them.
6. **Close the deal:** Customers are risk-minimizing and often skeptical of new products or reluctant to make decisions. Therefore, the customer typically needs a small push or "call to action" to commit. The methods are many. For example, it can be mentioned stocks are limited or the offer only applies this month, or questions that imply the deal is taken for granted can be asked, such as "Do you want a silver or gold subscription?" or "When would you like the subscription start?"
7. **Follow up:** Uncertainties will exist at the beginning, and the customer should feel appreciated and reassured that the right choice is made to ensure customer satisfaction in the after-sales evaluation that a customer always makes, whether conscious or unconscious. In this phase, the task is to complete the current sale in a satisfactory manner, and at the same time, creating the foundation for future sales and long-term development of customer relations.

HOW CAN YOU USE THE MODEL?

The model provides a common conceptual framework and reference in daily communications about a company's sales. The model can be used as a basis for the organization of effective sales and as a checklist for which tasks should be solved in each phase. In addition, the model can be used to analyze or evaluate specific sales processes, highlighting what was successful and what did not go well, and what we can learn, etc. Finally, the model demonstrates significant checkpoints for the skills an efficient salesperson should possess or learn.

WHAT ARE THE SHORTCOMINGS AND WEAKNESSES OF THE MODEL?

The model does not provide answers about how to arrange a meeting with the customer, which represents a significant challenge.

In addition, the model is about a single sale, and not about the customer relationship, which is the goal. In other words, the model illustrates a situation where a sale is made to a new customer. This is, of course, a crucial first step, but only touches the surface in customer relations. The model does not describe how to develop and maintain customer relations after the first sale.

It is also implicit in the model that the purchase is of significant importance for the customer and that the sale is performed at a personal meeting. When a customer purchases goods of smaller or moderate amounts, they usually choose to purchase over the internet, email or by phone, rather than to invest precious time in a personal meeting. For purchases without personal meetings, e.g., e-business, the course is a little different. However, most points, especially 3 to 7, are always relevant, no matter how the sale takes place. For example, it is apparent that the points are always incorporated into a good webshop.

Last but not least, the model does not take into account cultural differences in the manner in which we act in direct meetings with trade partners which can be significant.

REFERENCES

Andersen, Finn Rolighed, Bjarne Warming Jensen, Mette Risgaard Olsen et al. (2015). *International markedsføring*, 5th edition. Copenhagen: Trojka.

Buch-Madsen, Kim (2005). *Marketing – klart og koncentreret*. Frederiksberg: Samfundslitteratur.

Jobber, David & Fiona Ellis-Chadwick (2016). *Principles and Practice of Marketing*, 8th edition. Maidenhead: McGraw-Hill Education.

Zappulla, Justin & Nick Kane (2016). *Critical Selling: How Top Performers Accelerate the Sales Process and Close More Deals*. New Jersey: John Wiley & Sons.

SALES MANAGEMENT
By Michael Sjørvad

INTRODUCTION

This model gives an overview of the sales manager's tasks regarding organizational and management assignments.

WHAT IS THE MODEL ABOUT?

The model gives a general description of a sales manager's duties, based on the company's overall strategy, including the marketing strategy. The sales manager's work is divided into two main groups; sales organization and sales management.

Sales Organization: The size of the sales force is determined by the amount of work per customer, which is defined by several factors, such as customer complexity, customer size, sales efforts, and the desired relationship with the individual customer.

Design of a sales organization can generally be performed in three ways and is in relation to geographical areas, product specialization, and a customer-oriented approach.

The *geographic* sales organization is allocated based on sales potential and workload, and sellers are responsible for selling all products in the assortment. The geographical breakdown is more cost-effective than the other two methods, and this division contributes positively to the development of close relationships between the seller and the buyer. On the other hand, the seller must handle a wide range of customers and products at the expense of detailed insight.

If the company has developed a differentiated product range that targets many different groups, the company may consider dividing the sales force based upon *product specialization*. This division ensures a high level of product knowledge in the salesperson but can lead to increased transportation costs, and the customer may experience overlap between the company's various sellers.

A *customer-oriented* approach may be preferable if the purchasing behavior is very complex and requires the participation of many different functions and departments throughout the value chain. A Key Account Manager (KAM) fulfills this role that focuses on closer relationships, and the KAM "draws" the order throughout the organization. However, this approach places great demands on the seller's understanding of the company's and customer's value chains, and this organization can lead to increased transportation costs.

Sales Management: Apart from setting sales goals, developing sales strategies, and compiling the right sales organization, the sales manager must set personal sales goals, recruit, train, and motivate salespeople.

Determining goals: The sales manager must break down the overall sales goals to team goals or individual sales goals for the individual sellers, but it may also be a combination of these. The goals can be quantitative or qualitative. For example, quantitative targets can be divided into input targets (number of customer visits, number of calls), output targets (sales in DKK or units), and hybrid targets. Hybrid targets are a combination of input and output goals (sales per visit). The seller may be involved in the targeting process, thereby increasing motivation and commitment.

Recruitment and selection: The importance of recruiting the "right" sellers cannot be overestimated and should be based upon a fixed recruitment procedure founded on the company's values and culture, as well as job descriptions. The final selection is based upon a mix of general sales skills and talents, as well as personality traits that translate well with customers, the position, and business values.

Training and development: The scope and depth of training depend upon the seller's knowledge and experience and should include: company goals, strategies and organization, products, competitors and their products, sales procedures, sales techniques, communications and relationships with stakeholders. The education should be followed by a customized course in the "field" where the sales manager and/or course manager provide feedback on customer visits.

The sales manager must continuously develop and train the seller based on an assessment of the seller's performance, strengths, and weaknesses. The manager should help the seller identify and take advantage of their strengths, minimize weaknesses, and monitor progress and development.

Motivation and rewards: Putting together the right reward system can be difficult, as people are motivated by many different factors, such as values, personality, and money. Successful sales managers increase the motivation of each seller, and may, for example, translate motivational theories into individual and practical behavioral goals or performance goals. Performance salary often has a degree of commission and/or bonus plan, constructed either individually, team-based or as a mix.

Follow-up and evaluation: It is necessary to follow up on the goals set by the seller with praise and acknowledgment and provide ways to improve in order to reach goals – otherwise it may seem meaningless and demotivating to the seller.

HOW CAN YOU USE THE MODEL?

The model gives an overview of the sales manager's role and tasks in the interaction between the company's overall strategies, marketing strategies, and sales strategies.

The model provides the new sales manager with an overview of a sales manager's tasks and functions in main areas. The model can also give the experienced sales manager a number of points of reference when they to reflect on their own practice.

Furthermore, the model can be used to carry out an analysis of the company's sales management.

WHAT ARE THE SHORTCOMINGS AND WEAKNESSES OF THE MODEL?

The model is very simplified. The reality and everyday life of a sales manager are far more complex and consist of a nuanced interaction between sales and management, ranging from a strategic to an operational level.

The model gives a rough outline of the sales manager's tasks and functions in relation to the individual sellers and the organization but does not indicate much about how the individual sub-tasks are solved.

Sales management is far more than goal fulfillment and procedures, as the sales manager's function includes many interrelational tasks and functions in the sales department. In addition, the sales manager has other roles and functions outside the sales department.

Another aspect the model does not touch upon is the type of sales and the sales task in relation to the size and internationalization of the company.

Finally, the reader can be led to believe that sales management is a linear process rather than a circular process, with continuous adjustments and changes in the preceding areas in a continuous process.

REFERENCES

Jobber, David & Fiona Ellis-Chadwick (2013). *Principles and Practice of Marketing*, 7th edition. Maidenhead: McGraw-Hill Education.

Kotler, Philip T., Kevin Lane Keller, Mairead Brady et al. (2012). *Marketing Management*, 2nd edition. Upper Saddle River: Pearson/Prentice Hall.

4. STRATEGY AND INNOVATION

BOSTON/BCG MODEL
By Kim Buch-Madsen

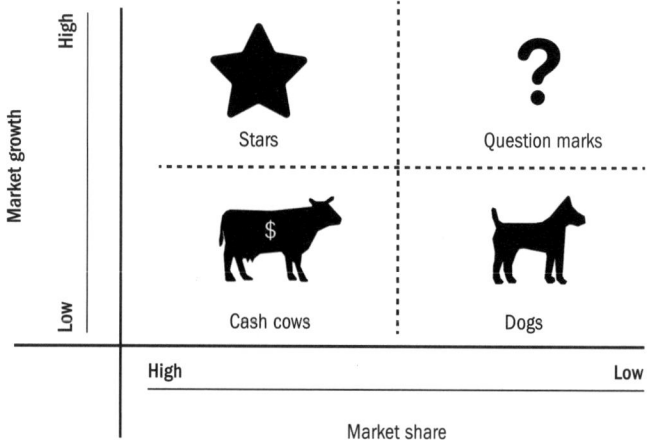

INTRODUCTION

The model provides an overview of a company's portfolio balance of Strategic Business Units (SBUs) or products, depending on whether they have high or low market growth and high or low market share relative to the largest competitor. The placement of the SBUs indicates which of them generate a positive and which a negative cash flow, while also indicating future opportunities because the model assumes Product Life Cycle for all SBUs/products.

WHAT IS THE MODEL ABOUT?

Companies working with multiple products in multiple markets need a good balance in the portfolio. For the company, it is about prioritizing their limited resources and distributing them between SBUs with short-term earnings and SBUs with long-term potential. An SBU is usually defined as an area of activity with a distinct market and financial structure and is typically a product category or product.

The Boston model shows a company's balance or imbalance in the portfolio, depending on the distribution between cash cows, stars, question marks, and dogs. An attractive portfolio consists of mostly stars and cash cows, some question marks, and few to no dogs.

The vertical axis of the model shows the market's annual growth rate, while the horizontal axis indicates relative market share to the largest competitor. It should be emphasized this is *relative* market share. The Boston model assumes that the company's products follow the Product Life Cycle (PLC) curve, where markets are born, grow, mature, and sooner or later fall. The model also rests on the fact that market shares and competitive positions are always in motion. Market leaders can quickly lose their position to competitors, especially in markets with rapidly growing technological development.

Question marks are SBUs in high-growth markets with low market share. They require a great deal of capital, e.g., product development, market communication and the development of distribution channels to follow a growing market and gain market share.

Stars are SBUs where a company is the market leader in high-growth markets. It is, of course, a desirable position that the company should attempt to achieve. However, it also requires a great deal of capital, e.g., capacity expansions to keep up with the growing market, and for marketing to defend the market leadership position, so cash flow is moderate and may even be negative.

Cash cows are SBUs that are market leaders in a low-growth market. They generate a great deal of cash flow because it does not require as much capital to maintain market leadership in a mature market.

Dogs are SBUs with a low market share in falling markets and should mostly be phased out by sale, abolition or gradual withdrawal. There are situations, however, where it might be a good strategy to stay and milk the last pockets in the market because competitors have pulled out or attractive niches remain in the market, even though the overall market is falling.

HOW CAN YOU USE THE MODEL?

The Boston model is relevant to companies that work with multiple products in multiple markets, typically companies of a certain size.

First, the development of the model stimulates systematic, strategic thinking and the company's internal dialogue about the future.

Second, the model provides a strategic overview of whether the company has a healthy portfolio, i.e., whether there is a balance between short-term earnings (cash cows) and long-term development (question marks and stars).

Third, the individual SBUs placement in the portfolio gives an idea of what would be a reasonable strategy, even though the model itself does not indicate concrete strategies. For example, you usually invest capital generated by cash cows in question marks so they can turn into stars, or in stars so they can become cash cows. According to the model maker, Bruce Henderson, cash flow must never be reinvested in cash cows.

WHAT ARE THE SHORTCOMINGS AND WEAKNESSES OF THE MODEL?

The model is highly simplified with its one-dimensional definition of market attractiveness and competitiveness. The attractiveness of the market lies in many factors other than growth, and competitiveness is much more than relative market shares.

The limits for high/low growth and high/low market share are unclear and can be debatable. Some textbooks set 7 % as the boundary between high or low market growth, and relative market share above 1 as the boundary between high and low market share.

Other textbooks set no limits and leave it up to the user himself. Bruce Henderson's original article about the model set no bounds but left the choice to the user/company. Users of the model must, therefore, set their own limits in relation to business and market or, at the very least, be critical to the limits set by others. Is market growth percentage below 7 % low? It greatly depends on the market. Also, if "large" market share requires a relative market share of more than 1, and the number two in the market with a relative market share of, i.e., 0.9, then, according to the model, the number two in the market has "low" market share. The accuracy of that can be certainly be challenged.

In addition, the model only includes products that are introduced into the market, but not products that are still under development. This is a significant shortcoming in today's business environment because innovation is an important strategic factor in most markets, and quick development and response rates can be as important as large market share.

Finally, the model does not consider the relation between SBUs, and it underestimates organizational aspects. For example, it could be the SBU's proprietary interests and incentives to manipulate data to get an attractive place in the model, avoiding the phasing out or down prioritization, which in practice means firing, cropped budgets, and reduced internal status.

REFERENCES

Andersen, Ole E., Svend Hollensen, Poul K. Faarup et al. (2016). *Moderne markedsføring*, 2nd edition. Copenhagen: Hans Reitzels Forlag.

Henderson, Bruce (1970). *The Product Portfolio*. BCG Perspectives, Boston Consulting Group. https://www.bcgperspectives.com/content/Classics/strategy_the_product_portfolio (retrieved 01.03.17).

Jobber, David & Fiona Ellis-Chadwick (2016). *Principles and Practice of Marketing*, 8th edition. Maidenhead: McGraw-Hill Education.

Johnson, Gerry, Richard Whittington & Kevan Scholes (2011). *Exploring Corporate Strategy: Text and Cases*, 9th edition. Harlow: Financial Times/Prentice Hall.

Reeves, Martin, Sandy Moose & Thijs Venema (2014). *BCG Classics Revisited: The Growth-Share Matrix*. BCG Perspectives, Boston Consulting Group. https://www.bcgperspectives.com/content/articles/corporate_strategy_portfolio_management_strategic_planning_growth_share_matrix_bcg_classics_revisited (retrieved 01.03.17).

ANSOFF'S MATRIX
By Kim Buch-Madsen

	CURRENT PRODUCTS	NEW PRODUCTS
CURRENT MARKETS	**Market Penetration** · Increase consumption per customer · New ways to use the product · Win market shares from competitors · Increase prices	**Product Development** · Brand new products · Product improvements · New product features
NEW MARKETS	**Market Development** · New customer segments · New regions or countries	**Diversification** · Concentric diversification · Conglomerate diversification

INTRODUCTION

The model describes in which direction the company can go to achieve growth, depending upon whether the company will continue to work with well-known markets and products, develop new products, attack new markets, or diversify by developing new products into new markets.

WHAT IS THE MODEL ABOUT?

Most businesses want to grow and expand. Ansoff's Matrix describes four overall growth strategies and specific strategic options within each strategy.

Growth in the Ansoff Matrix means greater revenue turnover. Higher earnings are only achieved if growth is not attained at too high of a price and if returns exceed the investments associated with growth.

"Market Penetration" digs deeper into existing business areas and seeks growth in current products and customer groups. This is done by taking customers from competitors, increasing prices, stimulating increased consumption of the product category, or inspiring customers to use the product in new ways.

By "Product Development," knowledge of the market and customer needs is used to develop new products or improve the products you already have. Product improvement can be achieved through boosting quality, adding a new service or the development of new product features.

Continuous product improvements can be made to create growth or out of pure necessity to keep up with developments in technology, customer wishes, and to avoid loss of market share to competitors.

In "Market Development," an opposite path is followed by using your line of products to win new target groups or to move into new markets. Internationalization of companies is an expression of this strategy, even though market development is also taking place within its borders, e.g., when new target groups have been cultivated for the same products.

By "Diversification," the company must handle unknown activities, regarding both product and market. This can happen as concentric diversification with certain connections to previous activities building on specific company strengths like competencies, resources or technology to introduce a new product or enter a new market. It can also be as conglomerate diversification without any connections to previous activities.

Diversification entails a higher business risk that must be counterbalanced by a high return potential, although diversification may seem reasonable in relation to the classic investment principle of risk diversification.Research has examined and discussed a great deal about diversification and whether, in general, it should be advised or discouraged. So far, there are no conclusions.

Examples of great success achieved with diversification are the British company, Virgin, with Richard Branson at the forefront, as well as Danish company, Maersk, but there are also examples of companies that have been burned badly by diversification strategies.

A number of factors determine which growth strategies a company will end up choosing. Two must be emphasized in particular. The first is competence, especially in relation to competitors. Typically, one chooses growth strategies well aligned with core competencies. For example, technologically advanced companies will often choose product development strategies, while companies with strong marketing skills will lean more on market development. Another crucial factor is business risk, i.e., losing money or tarnishing your reputation by failed activities. In any growth strategy, the company will, therefore, examine the potential profit value in relation to the risk involved.

HOW CAN YOU USE THE MODEL?

The model shows there are plenty of options to choose from when a company wishes to grow, which is a significant strategic point. In addition, it can be used to analyze which growth strategies a given company follows or which growth strategies competitors follow. Finally, the model can be used as an idea or strategy generator for the development of concrete strategies or as a common reference when strategic opportunities are discussed in the company.

WHAT ARE THE SHORTCOMINGS AND WEAKNESSES OF THE MODEL?

Overall, the model can be criticized for having an unrealistic and optimistic perception of the company's terms. Ansoff's model only indicates offensive growth strategies, but not defensive consolidation, turn-around, downsizing or exit strategies. It is not always a sound strategy to seek growth, and excessive optimism is a very common cause for the collapse of dominant companies (for example, as Jim Collins shows in the book *How the Mighty Fall*).

In tough times impacted by economic trends, business circumstances, and competing conditions, a company can consolidate or cut back by putting investments on standby, phase out products or withdraw from difficult markets. These options can be the company's own choice or be more or less required, for example, by a bank or investors. In these situations, Ansoff's Matrix is not suitable.

REFERENCES

Andersen, Finn Rolighed, Bjarne Warming Jensen, Mette Risgaard Olsen et al. (2015). *International markedsføring*, 5th edition. Copenhagen: Trojka.

Andersen, Ole E., Svend Hollensen, Poul K. Faarup et al. (2016). *Moderne markedsføring*, 2nd edition. Copenhagen: Hans Reitzels Forlag.

Collins, James Charles (2009). *How the Mighty Fall: And Why Some Companies Never Give In*. New York: HarperCollins.

Jobber, David & Fiona Ellis-Chadwick (2016). *Principles and Practice of Marketing*, 8th edition. Maidenhead: McGraw-Hill Education.

Johnson, Gerry, Richard Whittington & Kevan Scholes (2011). *Exploring Strategy: Text and Cases*, 9th edition. Harlow: Financial Times/Prentice Hall.

PORTER'S FIVE FORCES
By Kim Buch-Madsen

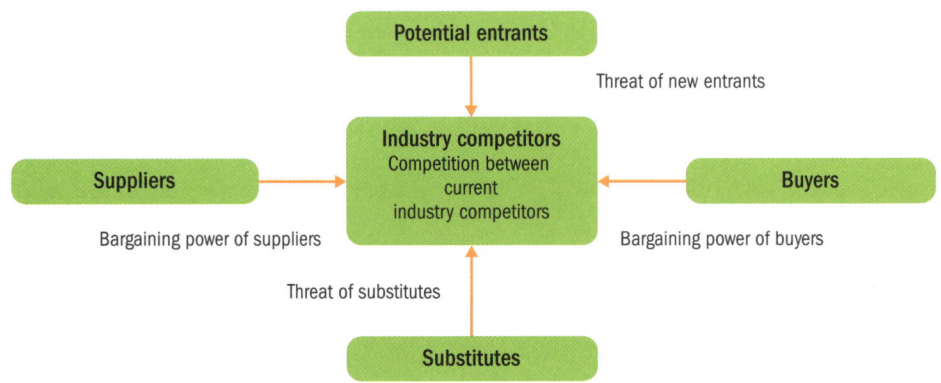

INTRODUCTION

Five Forces is about competition in a wider perspective of a certain industry, and not only applies to current competitors but also who could become competitors in the future. The company's suppliers and buyers are considered part of the competition. This is partly due to competition for growth or profit and control over important parties in the value chain, and partly because buyers and suppliers by forward or backward integration can become direct competitors.

WHAT IS THE MODEL ABOUT?

In Five Forces, competition takes place in three dimensions. The actual competition takes place in the middle "industry competitors" box. It also takes place in a vertical dimension with the threat of potential competition from new entrants and substitutes. Finally, the horizontal dimension demonstrates how profit and influence are shared with vendors and buyers, who also have the option of integrating forward or backward, thus, becoming direct competitors.

The model is named after the five competitive forces that comprise the competing players. However, the relationships between the five forces/players are equally important because it is in the relationships that industry players can influence the situation to their advantage. The five forces or players are current industry competitors, suppliers, buyers, potential new entrants, and substitutes.

The relationships between them are entry barriers for potential new entrants, buyer bargaining power, bargaining power of suppliers, competitive intensity between current industry competitors and the strength of threats from substitutes.

These factors determine competition and profitability in the industry. The connection between competition and profitability is the harder the competition, the harder it is to win customers, the lower prices you get, the more expenses you will have for marketing and production equipment, etc. to be a factor in the competition.

What factors cause entry barriers, competitive intensity, bargaining power, etc. to be high or low? According to Michael Porter, the factors called "determinants" do, as seen in the right column in the overview below.

These determinants are particularly important because this is where industry players are constantly trying to strengthen their position. This is where the model indicates strategic business opportunities for the company.

Entry barriers for potential new entrants	Economies of scale, capital requirements, access to distribution channels, legislation and political protection, differentiation, brand loyalty, expected responses from industry competitors
Competitive intensity between industry competitors	Equality in size and economic strength, stage of product life cycle, differentiation, capacity level (fixed costs share), the possibility of incremental capacity extensions, exit barriers, alternative utilization of production factors.
The strength of the threats from substitutes	Relative price/quality, switching costs, customer loyalty
Bargaining power of buyers	Size and degree of concentration in terms of industry competitors, product differentiation rate, product cost burden to customers, switching costs, the threat of backward integration, number of possible alternative suppliers
Suppliers bargaining power	Size and concentration level relative to industry competitors, shift costs, brand strength, the risk of forward integration

HOW CAN YOU USE THE MODEL?

The model has gained widespread popularity and has many ways to be used. The most common include:

- **Describe or analyze an industry:** The model is good for illustrating and understanding an industry, creating a (partial) image of own strengths and weaknesses, threats and opportunities, and to analyze.in which direction the industry moves.
- **Identify own as well as competitors' possible strategies:** The model can also be used to evaluate how the company can improve its competitiveness and position in the industry, what competitors might do, and how to make it difficult for potential new entrants to gain a foothold. The above determinants are the strategic tools the company can use to strengthen its own position in the industry and/or weaken its competitors.
- **Assessing the attractiveness of an industry:** Finally, the model can be used to analyze the attractiveness of an industry for companies outside the industry seeking new growth and "looking" into the industry. In this situation, questions such as how tough are the competition, how high are entry barriers, how much capital will it take to win and maintain a position are all considered. These are precisely the same questions that investors and banks ask when they

approve or not approve the decision to finance an entrepreneurial activity or to finance the growth of an established company into new industries.

When an industry's attractiveness is assessed from the outside, its features include:

ATTRACTIVE INDUSTRY	LESS ATTRACTIVE INDUSTRY
Low entry barriers	High entry barriers
Low exit barriers	High exit barriers
Suppliers and customers have low bargaining power	Suppliers and customers have high bargaining power
Zero to few substitution alternatives	Many and/or strong substitutions
Low competitive intensity	High competition intensity

Similarly, when the attractiveness of an industry is assessed by its current providers from within the industry, there is one significant difference, and that is entry barriers. As an established industry competitor you are not interested in low but in high entry barriers because you do not normally want new competitors to share customers and profits.

One of the qualities of the Five Forces model is it captures the competitive dynamics of an industry. In reality, industry is always in motion. There are always strategic games and counteraction in progress.

Therefore, it is crucial that you not only look at the "boxes" in the model but also in the relations between them. It is in the relations that the strategic game about competitive advantages takes place, and therefore it is here, the company can strengthen its position and weaken competitors.

WHAT ARE THE SHORTCOMINGS AND WEAKNESSES OF THE MODEL?

Five Forces do not include social perspective as, e.g., the PESTEL model's macro factors that affect the competitive conditions for both the industry and the individual company. In addition, the model sees competition as a zero-sum game where competitors are opponents and where one wins, and the other loses. Just as often, competitors work together. They can, for example, work together in trade associations, enter into strategic alliances such as education or technology development. They may be fierce opponents in one market, but collaborators in another.

Finally, Five Forces does not regard cultural, sociological and institutional conditions even though it may be of major importance in the industry. There may be cross-sector purchases and marketing collaborations as seen in the retail industry.

Most industries have trade organizations, and some are very powerful, such as the agricultural sector. Industries can have historically developed standards for what you do and do not do. Last, but not least, grassroots movements and NGOs can exert very significant influence. Global examples include Greenpeace and Occupy Wall Street, but also national and regional grassroots movements can exert significant influence. Finally, any industry is part of an institutional system where ministries and public agencies set the framework and can directly take action.

REFERENCES

Andersen, Finn Rolighed, Bjarne Warming Jensen, Mette Risgaard Olsen et al. (2015). *International markedsføring*, 5th edition. Copenhagen: Trojka.

Andersen, Ole E., Svend Hollensen, Poul K. Faarup et al. (2016). *Moderne markedsføring*, 2nd edition. Copenhagen: Hans Reitzels Forlag.

Buch-Madsen, Kim (2005). *Marketing – klart og koncentreret*. Frederiksberg: Samfundslitteratur.

Jobber, David & Fiona Ellis-Chadwick (2016). *Principles and Practice of Marketing*, 8th edition. Maidenhead: McGraw-Hill Education.

Porter, Michael E. (1980). *Competitive Strategy: Techniques for Analyzing Industries and Competitors*. New York: Free Press.

PORTER'S GENERIC COMPETITIVE STRATEGIES
By Christian Grandjean

	COMPETITIVE ADVANTAGE	
	Low cost	Uniqueness
Broad	Cost leadership (low price)	Differentiation
Narrow (niche)	Focused strategy (low price)	Focused differentiation

COMPETITIVE SCOPE

INTRODUCTION

The model describes four overall competition strategies from which a company can choose to gain competitive advantages in the market. It requires the company to make a number of choices. First, is the company will invest in low cost or differentiation as a source of competitive advantage? Second, will the company attack a wide market or focus on a small segment of the market?

WHAT IS THE MODEL ABOUT?

The model is based on two dimensions. Will the company:

- Compete at low cost with cheaper prices or differentiate by offering customers something unique or improved (competitive advantage)?
- Sell its products in a large or small part of the market (competitive scope)?

The company can ensure low costs, for example, by purchasing cheap, producing efficiently, achieving economies of scale, distributing efficiently or developing a whole new business model. The low costs will typically be reflected in a lower price. Differentiation takes place, for example, through design, quality, special services, high performance, fast delivery or a strong brand.

The second dimension of the model is about how much of the market the company wants to process, that is, whether the company will address a large or small part of the total market.

When combining the two dimensions of the models, four alternative competitive strategies will occur:

- **Cost leader (low cost, broad market):** The company offers services produced and distributed at low cost to a broad target group, typically, at a low price. Walmart and Burger King are examples of companies that are successful with the cost-leadership strategy.
- **Focused cost leader (low cost/narrow market):** Companies again market products that are produced and distributed at low cost but to a small target audience, for example, a localized, limited market or a limited segment of customers. An example is the operating system Linux.
- **Differentiation (unique or better services/wider market):** Companies that typically follow this strategy act differently, faster or better than competitors,

and offer something unique to a broad range of the market. The differentiation strategy requires that a company is able to convince customers about the uniqueness of product or service that their company provides. Differentiation is, thus always an experienced differentiation. As a result, market communication is usually an important part of the differentiation strategy, for example through clear communication regarding specific product benefits or a broader branding that makes the product or business attractive to customers. Companies with success in using the differentiation strategy are, for example, Nike and Apple.

- **Focused differentiation (unique or better services/narrow market):** This strategy is implemented by offering unique or better services, but only to a narrow market. Typically, services are tailored to the specific needs of a narrow target group. Examples of companies following this strategy are Tesla and Louis Vuitton.

The main point in the model is the company must choose one of the four strategies because they require widely different marketing, distribution, internal competencies, systems, etc. According to Porter, attempts to mix strategies and combine their mutual benefits will go wrong and lead to an unclear market profile, organizational confusion, and poor earnings. In Porter's opinion, you "get stuck in the middle."

HOW CAN YOU USE THE MODEL?

First of all, the model demonstrates that competitive strategy is about making choices. Businesses cannot be everything to everyone.

The model can be used as a framework to set concrete competition strategies in existing or new markets. Once the generic competition strategy is chosen, this will be part of the framework for product development, service concepts, distribution, market communication and the full range of action parameters/marketing mix (see 8 P model, page 56).

The model can also be used as a framework for understanding and analyze competitors' strategies and the direction in which a competitors' marketing mix is going.

WHAT ARE THE SHORTCOMINGS AND WEAKNESSES OF THE MODEL?

A shortcoming of the model is it does not operate with combinations other than the four established competition strategies. The model claims that companies cannot follow differentiation and cost management strategies at the same time, although the Blue Ocean model shows this combination can provide crucial competitive advantages.

In general, recent research has shown that competition strategies, cost management, and differentiation can be combined but also support Porter's theory that it is difficult and will not happen very often. If successful, gains can be huge though.

Companies that follow the two cost strategies must be aware of the increased degree of transparency that allows customers to compare prices online. These companies must, therefore, maintain the same price in all sales channels so that the strategy is not diluted by the possibility to purchase the product at one price in one place and at a lower price elsewhere.

It is important companies that follow the two differentiation strategies are aware of how they differentiate their products. On the one hand, the products must have unique features that customers find interesting so that they feel they get value for their money. On the other hand, the differentiation strategy does not mean that the company can ignore costs. Although cost is not the primary strategic focus, it must nevertheless be kept at a level where the differentiation does not become resource-intensive and consume the company's earnings.

Last but not least, the model is called generic competition strategies. This term refers to the fact that the model is general in nature. It certainly indicates four effective competition strategies but does not say anything about how they can be implemented specifically.

REFERENCES

Andersen, Finn Rolighed, Bjarne Warming Jensen, Mette Risgaard Olsen et al. (2015). *International markedsføring*, 5th edition. Copenhagen: Trojka.

Jobber, David & Fiona Ellis-Chadwick (2016). *Principles and Practice of Marketing*, 8th edition. Maidenhead: McGraw-Hill Education.

Johnson, Gerry, Richard Whittington & Kevan Scholes (2011). *Exploring Strategy: Text and Cases*, 9th edition. Harlow: Financial Times/Prentice-Hall.

Porter, Michael E. (1985). *Competitive Advantage*. New York: Free Press.

Porter, Michael E. (2004). *Competitive Strategy: Techniques for Analyzing Industries and Competitors*. New York: Simon & Schuster.

BLUE OCEAN STRATEGY
By Christian Grandjean

RED OCEAN	BLUE OCEAN
Existing markets	New markets
Well-defined industry boundaries	New definition of industry boundaries
Intense competition	Competition on new terms
Well-known rules of the game	New rules of the game
Focus on the strategic choice between differentiation or low cost	Focus on differentiation and low cost at the same time

INTRODUCTION

The Blue Ocean model focuses on how a company can make the competition irrelevant by creating or finding brand new markets by changing the rules of the game or offering something unique.

WHAT IS THE MODEL ABOUT?

The Blue Ocean model is an alternative to classic competition strategies, such as Porter's Generic Competitive Strategies.

Classic competition strategies focus on how a company can achieve a strong market position by beating its competitors in an existing market with well-known competitors, customers, and products. However, the struggle is difficult and demanding, among other things, as it is often easy to imitate products and services. According to the Blue Ocean strategists, fierce competition under these conditions colors the water blood red, therefore, the term "Red Ocean."

The Blue Ocean Strategy is vice versa the term for new markets, where it is neither sufficient nor relevant for a company to compete for a piece of the existing market. Blue Oceans are markets where the company stands alone without competitors.

To gain new profit share and growth opportunities, companies in Blue Ocean need to define new markets with new gaming rules, new competitive parameters, and unique products. Blue Ocean symbolize markets that do not already exist – a market without competitors, where the company's actions stand alone for an extended period without other companies imitating, and allow for new product demand.

According to the Blue Ocean Strategy, the journey towards new markets must take place through "value innovation." Value innovation is continually focusing on new opportunities by challenging existing thought and behavioral patterns. The goal is to discover new ways to develop, market, and sell a unique business product and, thereby, distinguish themselves from well-known competitors.

Value innovation is based on two dimensions. On the one hand, it is about creating new products and services that produce a unique, new value for customers and something the industry has not seen before. It is to discover what the customer wants before they realized they wanted it. On the other hand, it is also about reducing cost factors companies normally compete upon in traditional markets to attract customers, but are related to features not essential to the customers. The following figure shows the two dimensions and their interaction with value innovation.

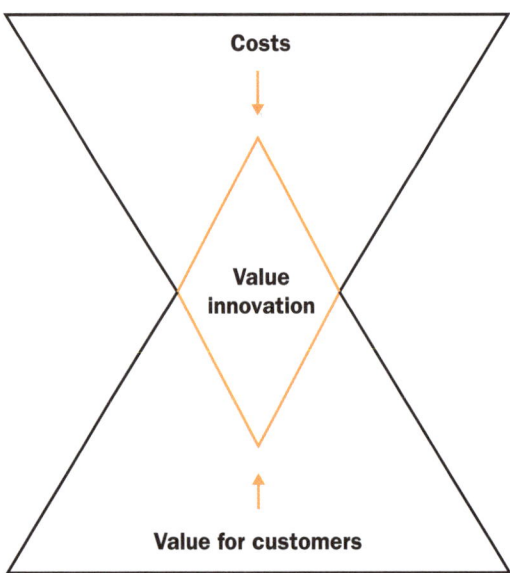

One example of a Blue Ocean company is the Australian winery Yellow Tail. They decided to take on the established wine houses and producers who traditionally market and sell wine in a way that requires interest and knowledge. Yellow Tail instead developed two simple products, a red wine and a white wine, whose flavour appeals to the masses. The two wines are sold in bottles with a contemporary and simple label which is distinctly different from the many other wines that are marketed in a language targeted at wine connoisseurs.

HOW CAN YOU USE THE MODEL?

The Blue Ocean model is an analysis tool that helps businesses to create and develop markets that do not already exist.

The model focuses on six overall parameters that companies can use to identify and develop new products into a new and unique business area. A number of sub-questions can be asked for each parameter, and the following are simply for inspiration:

- **Alternative industries:** Are there any products or services from other industries that can be used to differentiate the company from existing competitors?
- **Strategic groupings in the industry:** Many companies act similar to their competitors. Would it be of value to challenge what these groups of competitors are doing, or to do something different than competitors and think outside the box?
- **Purchasing patterns:** Would it create new opportunities if companies met customer needs differently than before, focusing on other stakeholders in the buying center or completely different customers?
- **Complementary products:** Is it relevant to supplement the company's products and services with other products that can add additional value?
- **Functional and emotional appeal to customers:** Would it be valuable to combine a product's functional values with an emotional appeal?
- **New trends:** What's new and what trends create new business opportunities?

WHAT ARE THE SHORTCOMINGS AND WEAKNESSES OF THE MODEL?

Blue Ocean markets are ideal but difficult to practice, especially when competitors are also looking for "Blue Oceans." Practice has demonstrated that it can be difficult for a business to be successful *alone* based on the Blue Ocean Strategy. However, many companies are getting more useful inspiration as well as new business in line with the Blue Ocean mindset.

It is important to be aware that markets are not static. When a business has been successful in a Blue Ocean market, it will not be long before a competitor surfaces. Therefore, it is important to continuously work on value innovation to challenge traditional thinking and explore new markets.

REFERENCES

Andersen, Finn Rolighed, Bjarne Warming Jensen, Mette Risgaard Olsen et al. (2015). *International markedsføring*, 5th edition. Copenhagen: Trojka.

Andersen, Ole E., Svend Hollensen, Poul K. Faarup et al. (2016). *Moderne markedsføring*, 2nd edition. Copenhagen: Hans Reitzels Forlag.

Kim, W. Chan & Renée Mauborgne (2005). *Blue Ocean Strategy – de nye vinderstrategier*. Copenhagen: Børsens Forlag.

Kim, W. Chan & Renée Mauborgne (2015). *Blue Ocean Strategy, Expanded Edition: How to Create Uncontested Market Space and Make the Competition Irrelevant*. Boston: Harvard Business Review Press.

BUSINESS MODEL CANVAS
By Kim Buch-Madsen

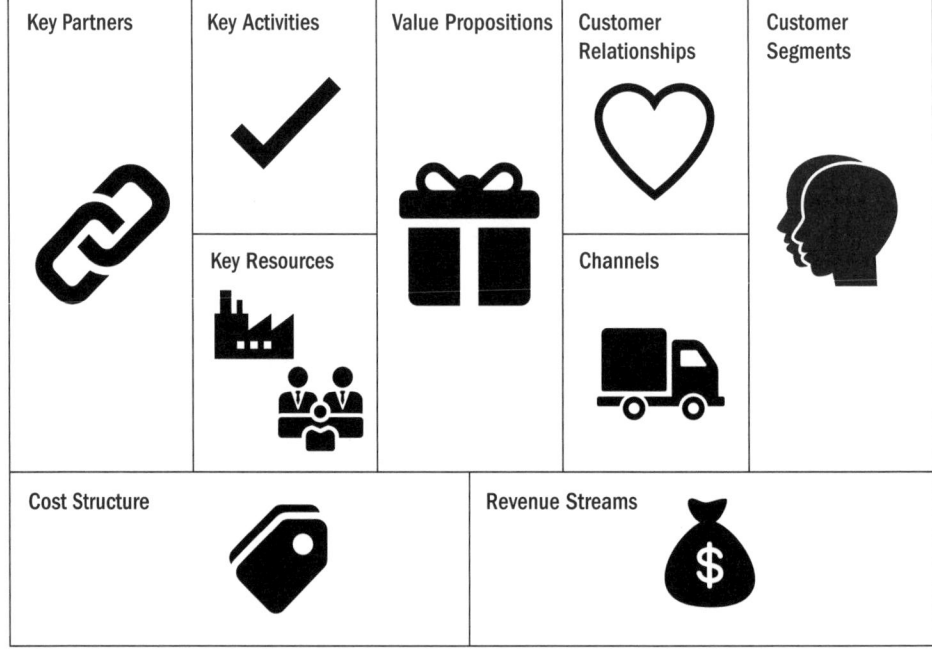

INTRODUCTION

The model shows which building blocks are part of a business model, and it can be used to understand, describe, analyze, and develop companies' strategy and innovation.

WHAT IS THE MODEL ABOUT?

Osterwalder's Business Model Canvas contains nine building blocks for business models; each block represents a key element of the business. In general, the model shows what a company delivers to whom, the internal architecture and the cash flows a company generates in terms of revenue and costs.

Although the model does not contain a specific order for how the building blocks are followed, the creators of the model, Alexander Osterwalder and Yves Pigneur, indicate the following order in their book *Business Model Generation* (2010). They also give examples of which elements are considered in each of the nine building blocks:

1. **Customer segments and target groups:** How does the company segment the market and which target groups do they choose to target?
2. **Customer value/value proposition:** What elements are included in the value package offered to customers to help them achieve, or avoid a problem or situation (need satisfaction or problem solving)?
3. **Channels to customers:** How do you reach out to the customers, both in terms of sales channels and distribution, and communication in the form of promotional activities?
4. **Customer relations:** How are positive, profitable relationships with customers established, developed, and maintained? Direct personal service, self-service, online trade, co-creation? And do you focus building and maintaining many short-term or fewer long-term customer relationships?
5. **Revenue streams:** Where does the money come from and how? Sales, subscriptions, royalties, rent, licenses? Fixed or variable prices?
6. **Key resources:** On which physical, financial, human and intangible assets are the business based? Intangible assets can be for example patents, technologies, databases or brands.
7. **Key activities:** What core tasks does it require to deliver the value package to

the customer, for example, design, development, production, service, delivery, hotline, web platforms?
8. **Key partners:** In what cooperation agreements, strategic alliances and joint ventures are the company engaged, for example in the areas of product development, distribution, sales or education, and with what motivations?
9. **Cost structure:** What fixed and variable costs do the business activities generate, which cost items weigh heaviest, where is the breakeven, which economies of scale and other cost drivers are strategically crucial?

The Business Model Canvas provides elements and concepts to understand a company's overall strategy and marketing efforts, how marketing is related to other activities in and outside the company, as well as the revenue and cost structure it all activates. At the same time, the model shows the elements an entrepreneur should consider when establishing his business and the elements an established company can change or modify to innovate.

HOW CAN YOU USE THE MODEL?

The model can help companies to understand, analyze, develop, and innovate. It provides a solid understanding of a company's business and how marketing and customers are part of the overall plan. It includes the underlying structure that creates the value package for which a customer pays, how a company organizes and delivers the value package and interacts with customers, as well as what revenue and costs it generates.

In study assignments, the model can be used to describe a company's business model and in practical contexts, such as dialogues or maps for an organization's internal work. Analytically, the model can be used to compare different companies' business models or to analyze the strengths, weaknesses, and distinctive features of the company you are focusing on. It may be your own business, a competitor, a business partner, a business you want to buy, or a company you are considering lending to or investing in if you are a bank or investment company.

Finally, the model can be used to develop a new business from scratch. Established companies can also utilize this model to innovate in areas they want to get ahead in, composing or prioritizing the nine building blocks different from your competitors and/or developing new products and services.

The model is widely used to innovate. First, the structure of the nine elements is easy to understand and use; it also serves as a good visual tool. Second, business model innovations go deeper and are more difficult for competitors to imitate than innovations of single items, such as a particular product feature or marketing strategy.

WHAT ARE THE SHORTCOMINGS AND WEAKNESSES OF THE MODEL?

The Business Model Canvas primarily focuses on a company's internal operations. It does not include the industry in which the company competes or is to compete (see Porter's Five Forces, page 148), or the macro environment the company should function in (see PESTEL, page 14) that can lead to threats and opportunities to which the company must respond.

In addition, the model does not include competitors or competitive considerations. Therefore, it does not capture the value of seeing the business model relative to that of its competitors. For example, the customer usually has alternatives when considering how attractive the value package is and what they are willing to pay for it. They evaluate in relation to what competitors can offer. The same applies to the cost structure. Whether a cost structure is appropriate or not depends largely on at which cost competitors can deliver a competitive alternative (see Porter's generic competetive strategies, page 154).

The model is also a tool that can be used here and now and does not cover how the future could develop or how the company can or will adapt. That is a significant shortcoming given markets and competitors never stand still but are in constant motion.

Finally, the model does not include technological advancements – an important point of which to be aware at a time where many markets are highly technology-driven. Emerging technologies can revolutionize entire industries and very quickly incite serious problems for large companies or attract new, strong, unexpected players to the market.

REFERENCES

Andersen, Finn Rolighed, Bjarne Warming Jensen, Mette Risgaard Olsen et al. (2015). *International markedsføring*, 5th edition. Copenhagen: Trojka.

Andersen, Ole E., Svend Hollensen, Poul K. Faarup et al. (2016). *Moderne markedsføring*, 2nd edition. Copenhagen: Hans Reitzels Forlag.

Newth, Francine (2012). *Business Models and Strategic Management – A New Integration*. New York: Business Expert Press.

Osterwalder, Alexander & Yves Pigneur (2010). *Business Model Generation*. Hoboken: John Wiley & Sons.

ROGERS' ADOPTION CURVE
By Kim Buch-Madsen

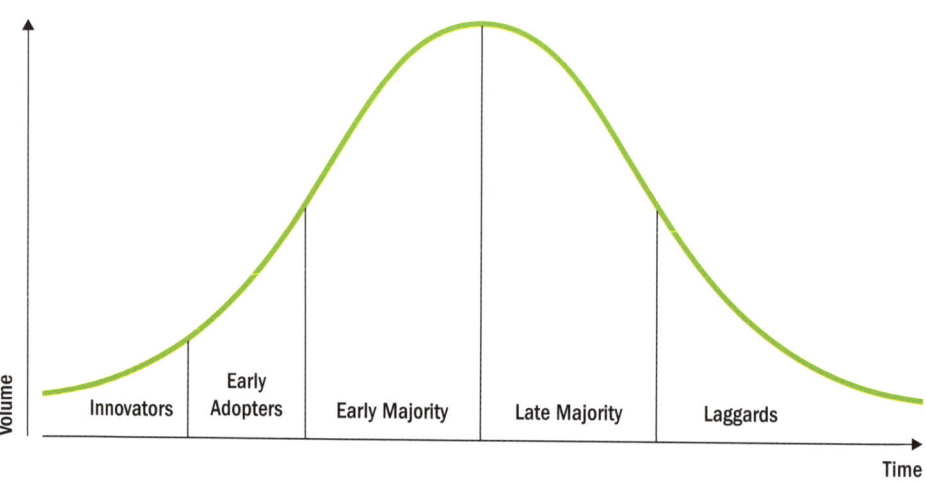

INTRODUCTION

The model is about how a new product is accepted and spread into the market. It is based on five customer groups and describes when and how rapidly different customer groups accept new products, and how large these customer groups typically are.

Finally, it describes how the majority segments mimic the behavior of early adopters, and why the first two groups are, therefore, crucial to the penetration of a new product and dispersion into the market. The term "new product" is used widely and can be any marketable innovation, whether it is a physical product, a service, an experience, etc.

WHAT IS THE MODEL ABOUT?

The model establishes common concepts as to how quickly and when different customer groups accept a new product. In addition, it provides standards for the size of the individual groups and describes typical behavioral features, motives, and other characteristics of the groups. The model demonstrates how most customers first accept something new once they have seen others use it or heard others recommend it. The exception is the first two groups of "innovators" and "early adopters" who are risky and confident enough to be the first, respectively. Therefore, these two groups are particularly important as a type of door opener to the market, although they are the smallest of the five groups.

The model is closely linked to the Product Life Cycle (PLC) model because it, among others, describes which customer types are typical of the individual phases of the PLC and which sociological dynamics are behind the PLC curve development in sales over time.

The model applies to both B2B and B2C markets and is structured around the following five categories of adopters:

CATEGORY	TYPICAL FEATURES
Innovators: Daring, risky	This group seeks the "excitement" of the new and unknown and are the first to try it. They are curious and cosmopolitan, often with international relations. They challenge the norms, do not seek the group's acceptance, and thrive upon the outskirts of their social communities. This group is financially stronger than the average and possesses a good technical understanding that makes it easier to begin new endeavors. When new products become mainstream, innovators lose interest and seek new challenges.
	Innovators are very few in number and do not seek to influence others. Nevertheless, the group is of great importance because they are the first to demonstrate new products or product uses and function in this way as door openers to the market.
Early Adopters: Respected, role models	While innovators live on the edge, early adopters remain key in their social communities, where they enjoy great respect and often are opinion leaders. They are self-confident, well-educated, and well-connected. As role models, others emulate early adopters or ask for their advice. They relinquish the role of being well-oriented and carefully assess before they recommend anything. Therefore, their acceptance serves as approval in the eyes of others. Early adopters are an extremely important group because of the respect they enjoy, and as role models, they are the connection to the rest of the market.
Early Majority: Conscious	The early majority make up about a third of the market, and their acceptance definitely opens access to the mainstream and mass market. They are a little quicker to comprehend new things than the average but are rarely opinion leaders. They are more mindful than early adopters. When the early majority accepts the product, it integrates into the culture.
Late Majority: Skeptical, careful	The late majority is less economically well-off than the early majority and has a greater need for security. They are motivated by what others are doing and need to see new products or services accepted in the group before adopting them. They are skeptical of new ideas, products and opinions and accept it only when the novelty and perceived risk are very limited.
Laggards: Traditional, old-fashioned	Laggards are the last to accept innovation, very rooted in the group and with a great need for security and traditional values. The past means a lot to them, and what is common is an important quality. They are suspicious of newness, partly due to limited financial resources. Laggards first accept a product when it is outdated, and something new is on its way.

When launching a new product, it is important to obtain quick acceptance from the first groups (innovators and early adopters) to rapidly spread to the remaining groups. Five product features serve as acceptance criteria that determine whether a product is accepted and spreads into the market and how quickly it occurs:

- **Relative advantage:** How is the perceived value compared to alternatives? How much better than existing products?

- **Compatibility:** How compatible is the product with previous habits, experiences, attitudes, norms, and needs?
- **Complexity:** How easy or difficult is the product to understand and apply?
- **Testability:** Is it possible to try or test the product and thereby limit the experienced risk?
- **Observability:** How visible is the product's benefits to others, how easy/hard is it to demonstrate and communicate?

These acceptance criteria are extremely important and at least as useful as the model itself. In most literature, they are described within the context of product development and innovation. Relative advantage and compatibility are the most important of the five according to Rogers' and others' research.

HOW CAN YOU USE THE MODEL?

First, the model demonstrates two strategic points in innovation, namely that different customer types carry sales at different stages of the penetration process, and that most customers initially will try a new product when they have seen others use or recommend it.

Second, the model shows which customer groups the marketing should be targeting when introducing new products. According to the model, targeting the two largest groups, though tempting, could be a losing strategy. Early majority and late majority together represent about two-thirds of the market, but they will never accept a new product unless they have seen others use it and heard others recommend it.

Therefore, "innovators" and "early adopters" are generally the target group for introducing new products because they are door openers and a bridge to the rest of the market.

Third, the model provides a rough, general description of the five groups of adopters, which can be used as a preliminary target group description or persona in the marketing.

WHAT ARE THE SHORTCOMINGS AND WEAKNESSES OF THE MODEL?

Most textbooks present Rogers' model with percentages, representing the size of each of the five groups. The figures originate from a research project about the spread of agricultural products in the 1960s, on which the model is based. However, there is no evidence these figures can be generalized, and thus the percentages are not included here.

The model is an ideal type of model, describing a general pattern and context that will often, but not always, follow the prescribed features.

The size of the groups may not follow the pattern of normal distribution as the symmetrical curve suggests. The curve may be steeper or flatter, depending on how fast the product is accepted and spread. It is also not certain that the individual groups have the size which the model demonstrates. The model does not indicate if and to what extent marketing can affect the five groups' acceptance of the new product, which is a significant weakness.

In addition, the model assumes that the same sociological mechanisms apply to the spread of innovation in both B2B and B2C markets. That contradicts big differences uncovered in other research.

The model has gained broad acceptance in research and classical textbooks but was originally based on the spread of six concrete innovations in agricultural societies in Colombia and the United States in the 1960s. Therefore, it should be used with caution and without the above-mentioned percentages.

REFERENCES

Buch-Madsen, Kim (2005). *Marketing – klart og koncentreret*. Frederiksberg: Samfundslitteratur.

Jobber, David & Fiona Ellis-Chadwick (2016). *Principles and Practice of Marketing*, 8th edition. Maidenhead: McGraw-Hill Education.

Rogers, Everett M. (2003). *Diffusion of Innovations*, 5th edition. New York: Free Press.

Tidd, Joseph & John R. Bessant (2009). *Managing Innovation: Integrating Technological, Market and Organizational Change*, 4th edition. Hoboken: John Wiley & Sons.

PRODUCT LIFE CYCLE (PLC)
By Kim Buch-Madsen

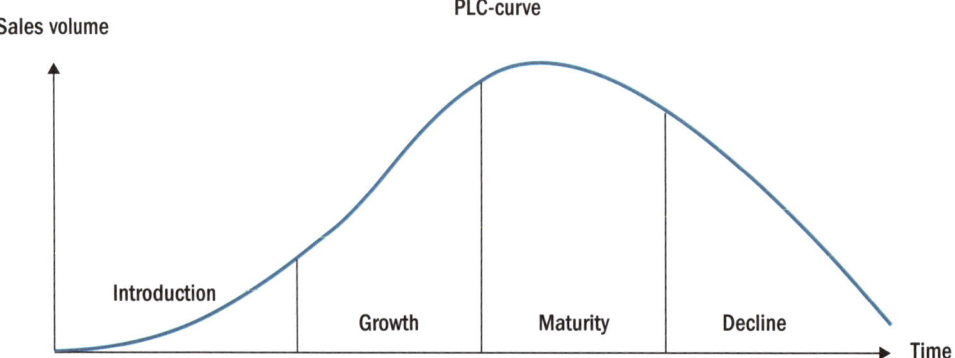

INTRODUCTION

This model demonstrates on a general level how sales of a product or product category can be expected to evolve by analyzing which market conditions will occur in different phases and how the company should strategically manage these conditions with portfolio planning.

WHAT IS THE MODEL ABOUT?

The model demonstrates that sales of products and product categories typically follow an evolutionary pattern. They are born, develop, and die as they are subsidized or replaced by new and improved solutions. This happens due to technological development, and development of customer needs and competitive conditions, all of which are strong underlying forces in any market.

The model's horizontal axis is time. The vertical axis is sales in volume.

PHASE	MARKET CONDITIONS
Introduction	The product is in its early stage, and sales rise slowly. There are only one or few providers that target demarcated segments, often innovators and/or early adopters, who are the first to try something new – see Rogers' adoption curve model, page 172.
	Earnings are limited or negative due to startup costs to establish awareness and sales channels.
Growth	Customers begin to accept the product, and sales increase quickly. With the addition of more providers, competition is increasing.
	With increased competition, positioning becomes more important, but the market continues to grow, so there is still room for everyone, attracting less professional providers, which may be harmful to the rest.
	Product improvement and expansion of sales channels are frequent strategies in the growth phase.
	Earnings continue to rise, despite large marketing investments, usually due to increased sales.
Maturity	Slowdown in sales that has peaked and started to fall a bit. Competition becomes intense because the market is no longer growing, and suppliers must solicit sales from each other.
	Therefore, price wars and marketing warfare is at its highest. In a mature market, everything that works is imitated, and therefore the need to differentiate products increases. Acquisition of new customers decreases or ceases, so distribution is intensified to reach all corners and margins.
	Earnings peak in the saturation phase where marketing investments accelerate. However, it declines at the end of the phase due to intensified competition and declining sales.

Decline	Sales decrease rapidly, causing some providers to pull out or close. If the exit barriers are high (see Porter's Five Forces, page 148), competition may still be fierce, but if low, few suppliers may have the remaining market to themselves.
	Price reductions and price competition dominate, and as marketing investments are reduced or ceased, competition in other parameters is often limited. Niche strategies are commonplace in this phase.
	Earnings are usually low or negative, but competition can be so diminished that some may earn a fair amount of the last "pockets" in the market despite declining total sales.

HOW CAN YOU USE THE MODEL?

PLC is a conceptual model that reminds us of several significant strategic points in marketing. First, growth rarely lasts forever, and will decrease sooner or later. That also means, most products over time reach a downturn where it is necessary to withdraw the product from the market or give it a more modest role in the assortment. It can be a big challenge if the company or dominant stakeholders have strong feelings or interests in the product or product category. The phenomenon is called "kill your darlings" in innovation literature (see the Stage-Gate Model, page 182).

Secondly, the model reminds the company that growth rarely lasts forever, so product planning is necessary. Strategically competent companies, therefore, plan to have products in different phases of the Product Life Cycle. If there are too many products in the growth phase, revenue and the future look bright. However, due to the heavy marketing investments that characterize the growth phase, earnings can be under severe pressure or the company can even be underperforming. Conversely, if there are too many products in the maturation phase, a great deal of money can be made here and now, but the future is threatened when the products reach the recession and the successors are not well planned. The Product Life Cycle model is closely related to the Boston/BCG model and can be viewed as the very reason why portfolio planning is necessary.

Thirdly, the model describes some "all things considered" guidelines as to what market conditions and marketing tasks *usually* occur in different phases, as well as anticipated earnings.

WHAT ARE THE SHORTCOMINGS AND WEAKNESSES OF THE MODEL?

Not all products and product categories follow the classic PLC curve. Very fashionable products or products with particularly rapid technology development can emerge more quickly, reaching a very short maturing phase, resulting in immediate decline. Others may be in a maturation phase for decades, without the sales curve showing signs of decline. Therefore, PLC must be strategically used as a principle model, which often but not always applies.

The model is very general, and it is difficult to define exactly when phases change. Therefore, the model is not suitable for concrete forecasts, although on the overall plan indicates how a market is likely to develop over time.

Finally, the model has been criticized for being a self-fulfilling prophecy. For example, if all providers heavily increase marketing investments because they believe they are in a growth phase, the product category sales will grow. On the contrary, if all providers decrease marketing efforts because they think they are in a recession, sales will naturally decline.

REFERENCES

Andersen, Finn Rolighed, Bjarne Warming Jensen, Mette Risgaard Olsen et al. (2015). *International markedsføring*, 5th edition. Copenhagen: Trojka.

Andersen, Ole E., Svend Hollensen, Poul K. Faarup et al. (2016). *Moderne markedsføring*, 2nd edition. Copenhagen: Hans Reitzels Forlag.

Blythe, Jim (2009). *Key Concepts in Marketing*. London: Sage Publications.

Buch-Madsen, Kim (2005). *Marketing – klart og koncentreret*. Frederiksberg: Samfundslitteratur.

Jobber, David & Fiona Ellis-Chadwick (2016). *Principles and Practice of Marketing*, 8th edition. Maidenhead: McGraw-Hill Education.

STAGE-GATE MODEL
By Kim Buch-Madsen

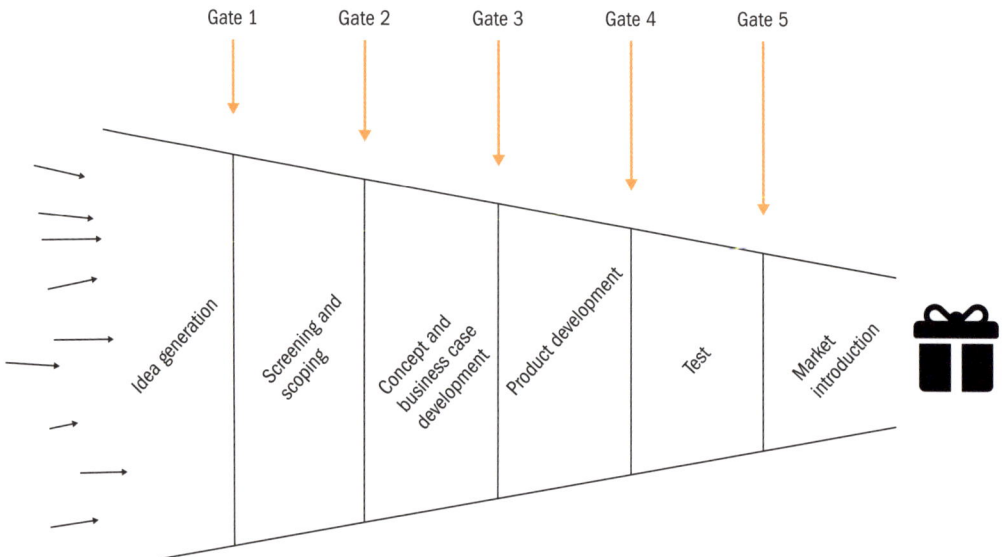

INTRODUCTION

The model demonstrates how companies typically systematize innovation processes in stages from idea to market with "gates" indicated to assess whether to proceed to the next phase, if something should be changed/improved, or if the concept should be eliminated.

WHAT IS THE MODEL ABOUT?

The model describes the stages product development and innovation typically undergo and the checkpoints ("gates") the concept goes through to qualify for the next level. Development is an expensive process where many ideas are sorted out along the way, and only a few make it to the market. Many business considerations need to be balanced; for example, the process should sort losing ideas from winning ideas, to ensure the highest likelihood of new products and services to be market successes, and also secure the fastest time to market. Last but not least, costs must be controlled, which tend to grow exponentially as the process evolves.

Variations of the Stage-Gate Model can be found in different sources, but the following stages comprise its core and will typically repeat:

1. **Idea generation:** Developing and collecting ideas. It is equally important to collect the ideas that occur by themselves in daily tasks, as well as ideas developed using creative techniques.
2. **Screening and scoping:** The ideas are assessed internally with relevant stakeholders. Some are ruled out; others are refined and improved.
3. **Concept development and business case:** Ideas are further developed into a form that can be tested with customers or those closest to the customers. The more the concept resembles a finished product, the more credible the concept test is. Business cases are prepared to assess whether a concept can be sold in sufficient volume and produced at competitive costs.
4. **Product development:** Further development of the concept to become a finished product or service. Typically, a large jump in costs occurs because both the product/service and delivery system must be developed.
5. **Test:** The product or service is tested under the most realistic market conditions possible. If it is not possible to test in a limited part of the market, a product test will typically be conducted with a sampling of potential customers.

6. Market introduction: The product or service is marketed to customers and retailers with the specific marketing tasks involved in introducing and incorporating something new.

Gates are the checkpoints where "stop" or "go" decisions are made between stages. A particular group makes the decision whether the concept will proceed to the next stage, or if something is to be changed, returned to the previous stage or stopped. Important questions are: Can it sell? Can it technically be produced/delivered? Will it be too expensive? Does the organization have the necessary resources and knowledge? Is there management support? Participants in the group must have the necessary powers to decide "stop" or "go." In addition, the team must ideally possess the following skills:

- Experience with innovation and product development
- Expertise in subject areas that are crucial in each case, for example, market analysis, technical production or cost budgeting
- Powers to add or remove funding
- Deep understanding of the company's strategy and business
- Objective and neutral stance in power struggles within the organization.

HOW CAN YOU USE THE MODEL?

The model gives an understanding of how and why companies construct systematic procedures for development processes and how many considerations should be balanced. In addition, the model demonstrates how a concrete development process can be designed and provides a conceptual framework for analyzing a particular company's product development and innovation. Finally, the model acts as a common frame of reference in the company's work on product development and innovation.

The model should be used as a rough outline indicating more actual activities than the model suggests. For example, it is common to market test as much as possible and not just once from a "test early, fail fast, fail cheap" approach, in which early, informal, and preliminary customer assessments are incorporated from the start.

WHAT ARE THE SHORTCOMINGS AND WEAKNESSES OF THE MODEL?

First, the process can be designed in other ways outside the model, and the company will choose its own path, although there will usually be common denominators. Secondly, development processes rarely run as linearly and "properly" as in the model. Product development and innovation are complicated, and the error rate is high even for successful companies. Power games, resource struggles, and conflicts are common when new and old meet; creativity and order must balance, and free thinking is reconciled with necessary management.

Stagnation, "mess," backflow, and stages running together are normal, and development processes are usually characterized by momentary chaos. Finally, the systematic process itself can exclude ideas and concepts that might multiply the company's business but are beyond the company's current thought processes, strategy, and business model.

These are the so-called "disruptive" innovations that revolutionize or destroy entire industries. Because large and established companies grow into embedded patterns, disruptive innovations rarely come from them, but mostly from small or new players.

REFERENCES

Andersen, Finn Rolighed, Bjarne Warming Jensen, Mette Risgaard Olsen et al. (2015). *International markedsføring*, 5th edition. Copenhagen: Trojka.

Cooper, Robert G. & Anita F. Sommer (2016). Agile-Stage-Gate: New idea-to-launch method for manufactured new products is faster, more responsive. *Industrial Marketing Management*, 59: 167-180.

Tidd, Joseph & John R. Bessant (2009). *Managing Innovation: Integrating Technological, Market and Organizational Change*, 4th edition. Hoboken: John Wiley & Sons

5. GLOBAL MARKETING AND ONLINE MARKETING

FIVE PHASES OF INTERNATIONALIZATION
By Svend Hollensen

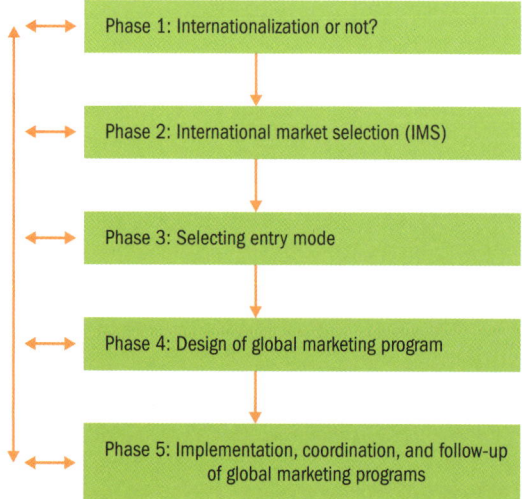

INTRODUCTION

The model demonstrates which phases are typically included in the internationalization process and what tasks the company will solve in each phase.

WHAT IS THE MODEL ABOUT?

The model applies to both B2B and B2C markets and is structured according to the following five phases:

PHASE	STANDARD FEATURES
Phase 1: Internationalization or not?	In a lot of industries, the domestic market is too small to generate long-term growth. Consequently, at an early stage a lot of SMEs will have to consider growth outside their domestic markets. This first stage is primarily for SMEs which have not yet been involved with exports and which still sell only to the domestic market. At some point, the company is confronted with an export opportunity, motivating it to decide whether it should begin exportation. The company must consider whether it possesses the proper skills (technical, commercial, linguistic, etc.) and financial resources to exploit international market opportunities. *Barriers/problems related to internationalization:* • Internal barriers/problems • Lack of sales resources • Lack of market knowledge • Problems identifying suitable import and export intermediaries • Language and cultural barriers • Problems obtaining knowledge about market conditions and conducting market analyses. *External barriers/problems:* • Trade barriers and technical trade barriers • Nationalist attitudes of customers/consumers.
Phase 2: International market selection (IMS)	The market choice is about identifying the most attractive international markets (countries) that fit the company's resource basis, establishing which international markets to choose and the order in which to pursue them. The market selection process differs depending on a company's age. Older companies generally show a tendency to export later on. In addition, they follow the so-called "sequential market selection pattern," i.e., a gradual expansion from nearby markets to distant markets at a moderate pace. These companies gradually build experience and a knowledge foundation that allows them to increase their expansion to more distant markets. On the other hand, younger companies, who often pursue internationalization sooner, tend to enter international markets more rapidly because they are export-oriented from the beginning and utilize their international networking contacts (e.g., to foreign suppliers or domestic customers with an international network). It is especially

	new companies (typically "Born Globals") who utilize the internet in the business model and develop a quicker internationalization strategy.
	If the internationalization occurs in interaction and partnership with other companies or if the company enters into a formalized network of companies, the company has the opportunity to be "pulled" into multiple markets without investing many resources.
Phase 3: Selecting entry mode	Once the choice of international market (or markets) is made, the next step is deciding the entry mode for top priority markets. This can be divided into three categories: • *Exports modes* (typically agents, importers or distributors): The degree of control for the manufacturer is lowest but at the same time flexibility is relatively high. • *Intermediate modes* (typically alliances, joint ventures, franchises, licenses): You reap the benefits of joining a local player who has a good knowledge of the local market. • *Hierarchical modes* (typically subsidiary companies): The manufacturer maintains the highest degree of control, but flexibility is relatively low because the manufacturer cannot change entry mode without losses in major investments already made.
Phase 4: Design of global marketing program	The company must develop its global marketing mix based on the 4 P model or the extended 8 P (see page 56). The company must decide what parameters it wishes to standardize across borders and what it wishes to adapt to the individual local market. As a rule, it makes sense to standardize "upstream" features (product development, procurement, production) and customize downstream features (marketing, sales, service).
Phase 5: Implementation, coordination, and follow-up of global marketing programs	The implementation and coordination of the global marketing mix depend upon the range of individual markets and customers. The company must decide which parts of the marketing mix should be centralized and organized from the headquarters (HQ) and which should be decentralized and managed via local partners or via subsidiaries. Sometimes, the company can benefit from Global Account Management (GAM), which in the short term is aimed at managing sales efforts towards global customers (GA = Global Accounts = Global Customers). The idea is the supplier can monitor their big customers with a global distribution network and use that network to become global more quickly than if the supplier has to internationalize individually. To determine whether the global marketing plan works, it is important the company continuously evaluates whether the individual marketing contributions of each country is maintaining the budgets the company initially set. Otherwise, the company may be required to correct the original marketing targets, for example, market share.

HOW CAN YOU USE THE MODEL?

The model can be used to evaluate how far a given business has come in the five phases. Some companies focus solely on the home market, and it is important for them to know what stages internationalization entails. If the company's hope is for success in internationalization, it must be approached in a structured manner, and strategic decisions must be considered in the proper order.

WHAT ARE THE SHORTCOMINGS AND WEAKNESSES OF THE MODEL?

The model is considered an ideal type of model, mapping out a general scenario. The actual path rarely or never matches exactly, though it usually follows roughly the described pattern.

The phases of the model reflect the company's shift from being home-oriented to internationally and globally-oriented. However, it is not certain that all companies will follow the model to the letter. For the so-called "Born globals" a jump in the phases might occur as these companies are global from the beginning of their existence. Maybe it is because they deliver an it-niche product or an internet-based product that can be sold globally, or they began as subcontractors to multinational companies who, more or less, decide in which markets to participate.

REFERENCES

Dyhr, Anna Marie, Steen Donner & Svend Hollensen (2009). *Internationale partnerskaber*. Copenhagen: Børsens Forlag.

Hollensen, Svend (2017). *Global Marketing*, 7th edition. Harlow: Pearson Education Limited.

In the above book, see pages 8-11 for a more elaborated visual of the five stages of the main models.

INTERNATIONAL COMPETITIVENESS
– FROM MACRO TO MICRO
By Svend Hollensen

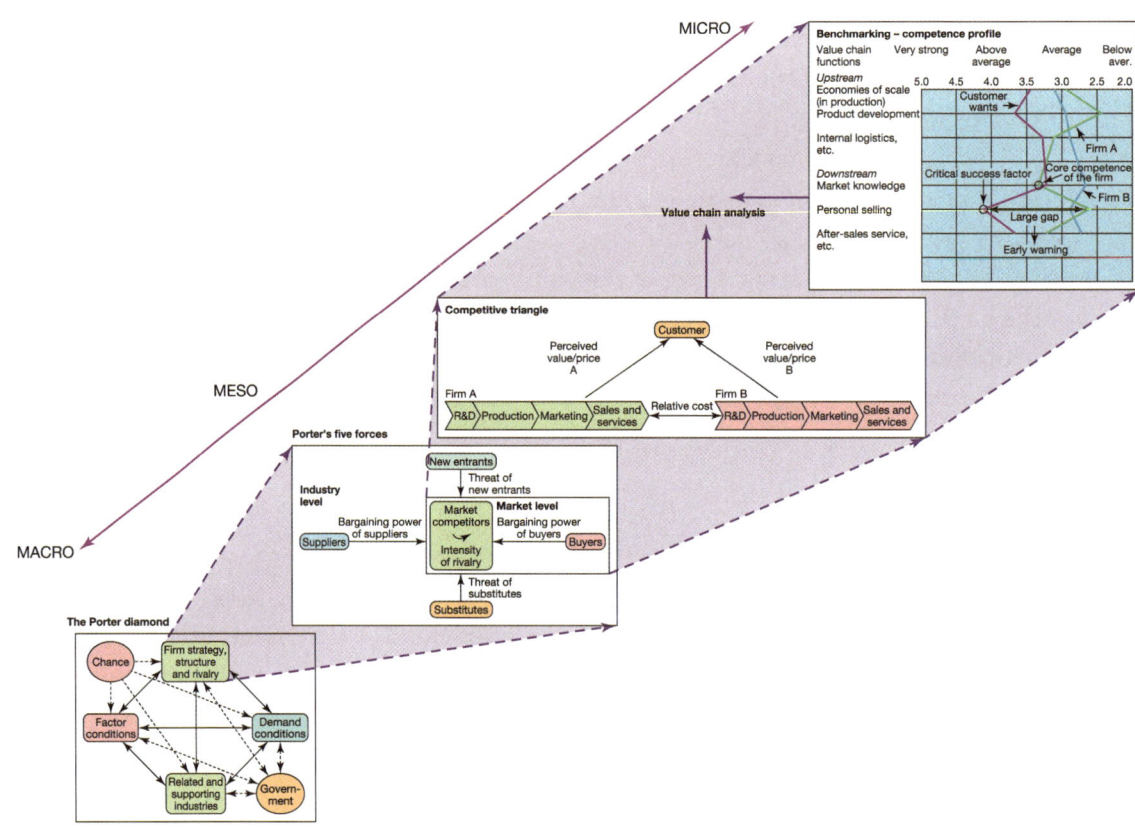

INTRODUCTION

The model shows a company's international competitive strength is complex and should be seen in a broader perspective using a range of models from macro (country level), across the meso (industry level) to the micro level. You begin in the lower left corner and move up to the upper right corner. The model works on the basis of a kind of "boxing" system. When you open the box, "Firm strategy, structure and rivalry," Porter's Five Forces model pops up and when you open "Market Competitors" and "Buyers," then the competition triangle opens up, etc.

WHAT IS THE MODEL ABOUT?

MODEL	TYPICAL FEATURES
Porter's Diamond	The competitiveness of a company depends to some extent on the characteristics of the country in which the company is rooted. The explanatory elements are: • Factor Conditions (the most mobile factors are technology and economic capital; the most important factor is probably "Human Resources"). • Demand Conditions (native country demand for the business products and services is of great importance to the company's international competitiveness). • Firm Strategy, Structure and Rivalry (the better strategy the company has, and the harder the domestic competition is, the better the company will be suited in the international market). • Related and Supporting Industries (when companies develop new innovative and advanced products and services, they need a network of domestic suppliers that are also motivated to be on top). • Government (can act as a catalyst and create demand for innovative products and services). • Chance (companies can be successful by random events that cannot be predicted or controlled).
Porter's Five Forces	Five Forces is about competition in a wider perspective of a certain industry, and not only applies to current competitors but also to those who could become competitors in the future. The company's suppliers and buyers are considered part of the competition. This is partly due to competition for growth or profit and control over important parties in the value chain, and partly because buyers and suppliers by forward or backward integration can become direct competitors.

Competitive Triangle	Shows there are two factors that determine who is successful in gaining customer favor: the perceived value that companies deliver to the customer and the level of costs it generates. Both the company and its competitors attempt to create the greatest possible value for the customers (relative to the price they should pay). However, customer perceived value is not the only factor that determines the "battle". In the long term, a company can only beat the competition if it can produce the product (and thus the value) at a cost level that is lower than its competitors (relative cost). Alternatively, it can win the match by delivering higher value, but at the same cost level as the competitor.
Benchmarking	Shows in detail how customers weigh different value chain features – both upstream and downstream – in relation to what is most important for a supplier to fulfill (customer wants/the violet graph). Then, the customer assesses how business A performs in relation to customer wants (the green graph) in addition to business B (the blue graph). For example, if we are business A, we can see (for personal sales efforts) there is a big gap between customer wants (requires high performance) and how we meet them. Since we are not quite good in that area (and less than business B), it can provide an "early warning," that to better meet the customer's strict wants, we really need to upgrade personal sales efforts.

HOW CAN YOU USE THE MODEL?

You can evaluate a company's international competitiveness in a broader perspective. The model is particularly good at explaining why some countries have industries where you have a competitive advantage worldwide. For Denmark, the model can be used specifically to explain how a small country can establish a wind turbine industry. Denmark is home to the world's largest wind turbine producers, such as Vestas and Siemens. In addition, Denmark is host to a whole "cluster" of subcontractors in the turbine industry, such as LM Windpower, one of the world's largest wind turbine blade manufacturers (bought by General Electric at the end of 2016). If the country does not constitute a competitive advantage within a specific industry, you can always skip the Porter Diamond Model and start directly with the Porter Five Forces analysis, then move toward the top right corner of the model.

WHAT ARE THE SHORTCOMINGS AND WEAKNESSES OF THE MODEL?

The model is considered an ideal type of model, mapping out a general scenario. The actual path rarely or never matches exactly, though it usually follows roughly the described pattern. Similarly, the model shows some relevant analysis types, but not how these analyses are performed.

In the benchmarking analysis, customers on the B2C market will normally not have deep insight into the company's or the competitors' upstream functions, making this analysis model suitable primarily for the B2B market.

REFERENCES

Hollensen, Svend (2019). *Marketing Management: A Relationship Approach*, 4th edition. Amsterdam: Pearson.

Porter, Michael E. (1985). *Competitive Advantage: Creating and Sustaining Superior Performance*. New York: Free Press.

Porter, Michael E. (1990). *The Competitive Advantage of Nations*. New York: Free Press.

Porter, Michael E. (2008). The Five Competitive Forces That Shape Strategy. *Harvard Business Review*, 86 (1): 78-93.

HOLLENSEN'S MARKET ASSESSMENT MODEL
By Svend Hollensen

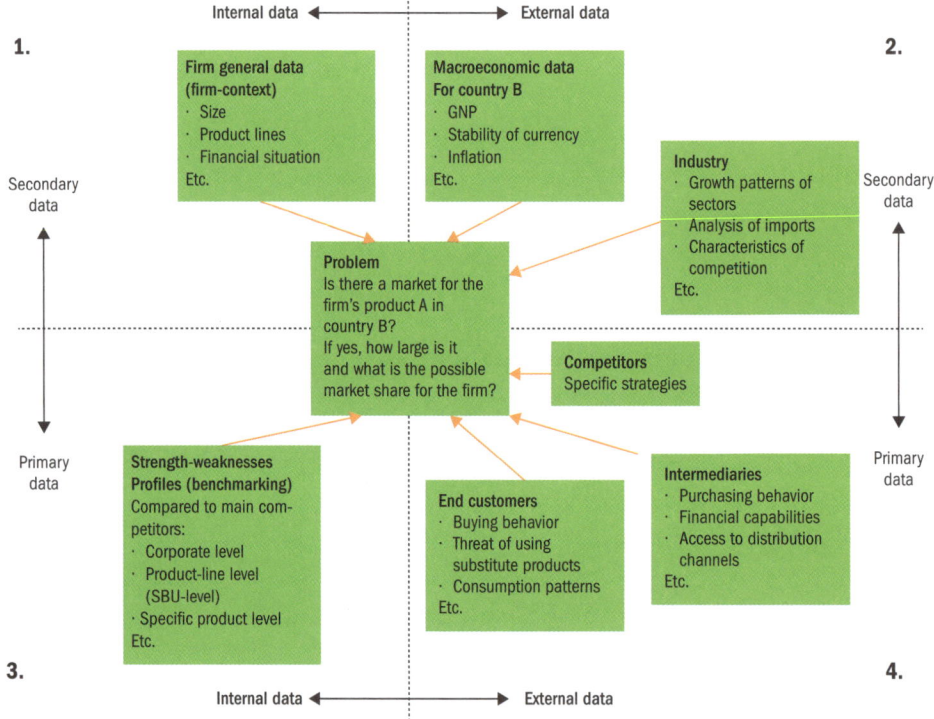

Categorization of data for assessment of market potential

INTRODUCTION

The model is used in market analysis processes when a company evaluates its market potential in a specific market, and it assesses what types of information are required to make this valuation. Similarly, the model also lists the order in which the information is to be collected.

WHAT IS THE MODEL ABOUT?

The model demonstrates four groups of factors and data that determine the potential of a given company's product in a specific market. The model indicates that there are two dimensions of data:

- Internal/external data
- Secondary/primary data.

This way, four groups of data, can each contribute to the question: Is there a market for our product in country X? How big is the market and what market share can we achieve in this market?

DATA CATEGORY	EXPLANATORY ELEMENTS (In terms of internal data, it is assumed analysts are outside the company because an employee/manager has immediate access to internal data)
Internal data/ secondary data	This data category provides a preliminary assessment of the type of business involved. Most companies have a website where basic information can be found, such as sizes, product types, services, international activities (e.g., company subsidiaries), and financial health.
External data/ secondary data	A country's macroeconomic data can provide a preliminary indication of market potential. This can be supplemented with more detailed industry data. The model purposefully situates this "box" closer to the primary data because the acquisition of this data can involve the acquisition of primary data, such as participation in exhibitions where personal interviews (talk with colleagues) can provide insight in terms of competition intensity of the industry in question.
Primary data/ internal data	To assess a company's competitiveness in a specific market, it is necessary to evaluate the competitiveness (strengths/weaknesses of competitors) based upon internal interviews with key individuals in the company (i.e., acquisition of primary data). These interviews can occur at the "corporate" level, at the SBU (Strategic Business Unit) level or a specific product level.

Primary Data/ external data	The "Competitors" checkbox is listed fairly close to the secondary data because general information about competitors may sometimes be found on the internet where there may be relatively easy access to competitor databases (possibly with payment for access). Regarding specific competitor information, this collection often involves specific interviews with customers and other players in the industry (possibly suppliers).
	Information about end customers and intermediaries' purchasing behavior most often involves obtaining specific primary data through personal interviews. This is probably the most resource-consuming part of the data collection.

HOW CAN YOU USE THE MODEL?

In general, the model can be used to obtain an overview or map of factors that can highlight the market potential and information required to succeed.

The model can be used to check whether all four data categories have been covered in the market assessment. The model also provides an indication of where to begin data collection and the order of the different data collection phases. The normal procedure is to start with one and then continue with two, three, and four.

It is common to begin where it is easiest to collect information and pick the low hanging fruit. From that point, you move into areas where data is more difficult to collect but also has greater information value.

WHAT ARE THE SHORTCOMINGS AND WEAKNESSES OF THE MODEL?

The model is a so-called ideal type model, which indicates there are four data categories necessary when analyzing a company's market potential in an international market. However, this does not always have to be the case. Of course, it depends on one's prior knowledge (if you are employed by the company in question, one's prior knowledge is much greater) and you can search for information specifically in those categories where there are weaknesses in the existing knowledge base. The model does not demonstrate all the relevant data types either, just the most important ones.

REFERENCES

Adiham, Phani Tej, Sampada Gajre & Shubhra Kejriwal (2009). Cross-cultural competitive intelligence strategies. *Marketing Intelligence & Planning*, 27 (5): 666-680.

Bell, Peter C. (2015). Sustaining an Analytics Advantage. *MIT Sloan Management Review*, 56 (3): 20-24.

Hollensen, Svend (2017). *Global Marketing*, 7th edition. Harlow: Pearson Education Limited.

FUNNEL MODEL FOR INTERNATIONAL MARKET SELECTION (IMS)

By Svend Hollensen

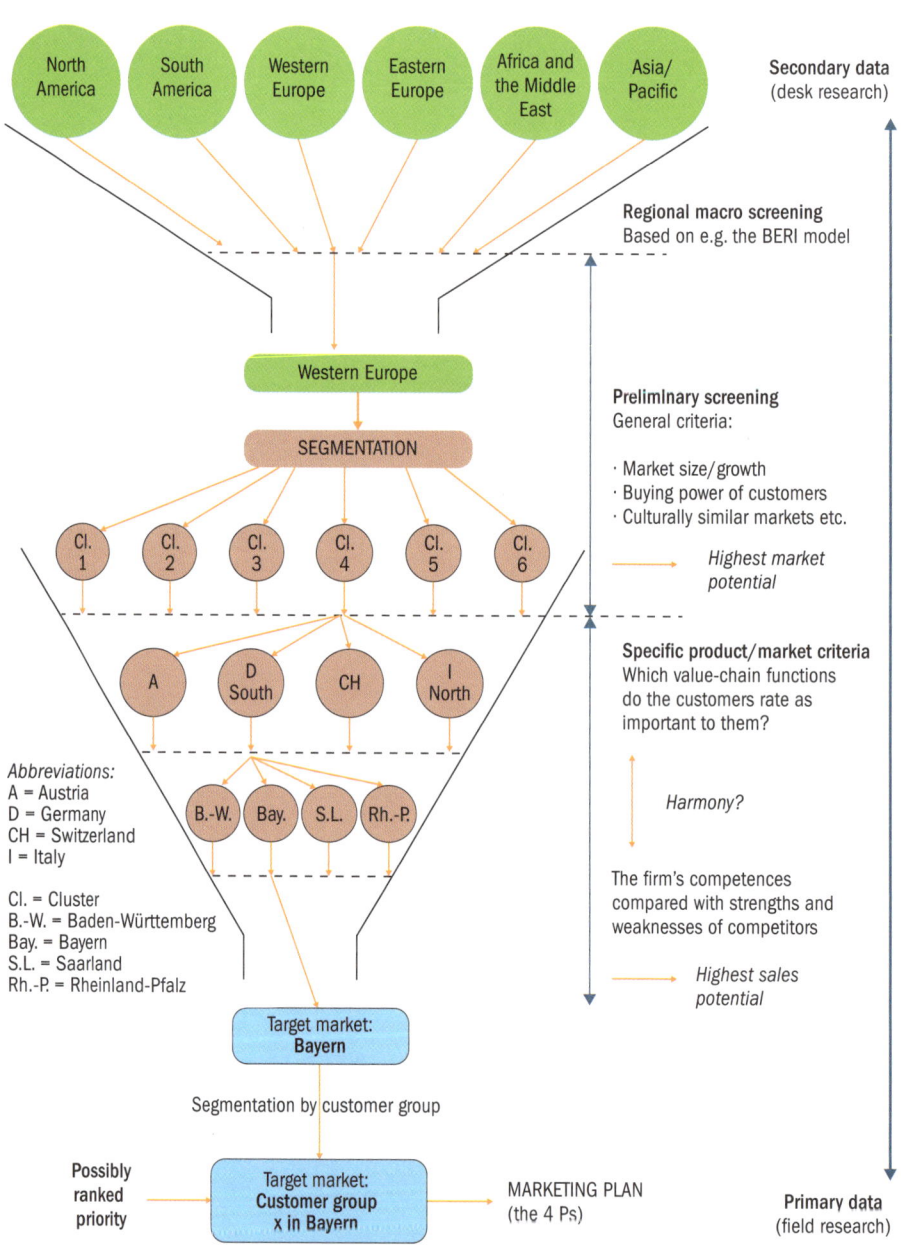

INTRODUCTION

The model demonstrates how to choose the most attractive markets to suit a company's competencies should it wish to expand internationally. To the right, the model shows what type of information (secondary or primary data translated into screening criteria) corresponds with a given level in the funnel model. The model shown is an example of the funnel model application in practice. In this case, the model recommends starting with Bavaria (in Germany).

WHAT IS THE MODEL ABOUT?

The model starts from the top with a coarse screening process, allowing all regions to enter the funnel. This phase is followed by a "fine-grained" screening of a more specific region further down the model and eventually concludes with a specific market choice, with subsequent development of a marketing plan for this market.

PHASES	TYPICAL FEATURES
Coarse (preliminary) screening	After a regional macro screening, additional screening is performed based on secondary data as it is the least resource-demanding method for generating relevant data. At this initial level, macroeconomic factors are typically used, such as GDP, GDP per capita, and population size. Different indices (e.g., BERI Business Environment Risk Index), which companies can subscribe to, have been developed to assess the business climate of different countries. In addition to BERI (publishing data from their index only upon payment), there are a few organizations that publish indexes for different countries' business climate (business risk), including macroeconomic indicators. Among these are Euromoney Country Risk (www.euromoneycountryrisk.com).
Fine-grained screening	Here, more specific criteria are used, based upon obtaining primary data, via personal interviews, which of course, can also be combined with the most relevant secondary data, such as industry reports. All of this data is intended to clarify, where (which country) is the best match between external market opportunities, internal strengths (competencies) and competitors' strengths and weaknesses.
Final market choice	The output of this screening process is a prioritized order of (typically three) countries, which the analysis has proven to be the most attractive markets. The reason it is important to have a priority order is that top management can often have their special reasons not to choose the highest-priority country. Perhaps locally, the company has acute personnel problems that cause priority number one not to be used. In the above example, it might mean that instead of the first priority being Bavaria, one would choose one of the other states in the cluster, e.g., Baden-Württemberg.

HOW CAN YOU USE THE MODEL?

The model can be used to help companies identify the best market in which to enter and the different phases of the funnel model provide an overview of the types of data integral in making this choice. The model showcases a company that has developed a product that can be sold worldwide and helps answer the question: where to start marketing?

WHAT ARE THE SHORTCOMINGS AND WEAKNESSES OF THE MODEL?

The model is an ideal type of model, describing a general pattern and context that will often, but not always, follow the prescribed features.

It will not always be relevant to utilize the model from the top down, for instance, if the company has already decided a particular region (e.g., Western Europe or Scandinavia) should be the target market. In such a case, of course, you should begin farther down in the funnel model, using a fine-grained screening from the very beginning.

The model includes rational factors that can be clearly measured. However, internal power struggles and cultural differences can also be screening criteria in the final market choice.

REFERENCES

Andersen, Poul H. & Jesper Strandskov (1998). International Market Selection. *Journal of Global Marketing*, 11 (3): 65-84.

Hollensen, Svend (2017). *Global Marketing*, 7th edition. Harlow: Pearson Education Limited.

Ozturk, Ayse, Eric Joiner & S. Tamer Cavusgil (2015). Delineating Foreign Market Potential: A Tool for International Market Selection. *Thunderbird International Business Review*, 57 (2): 119-141.

HOLLENSEN'S MODEL FOR "ENTRY MODE" CHOICE

By Svend Hollensen

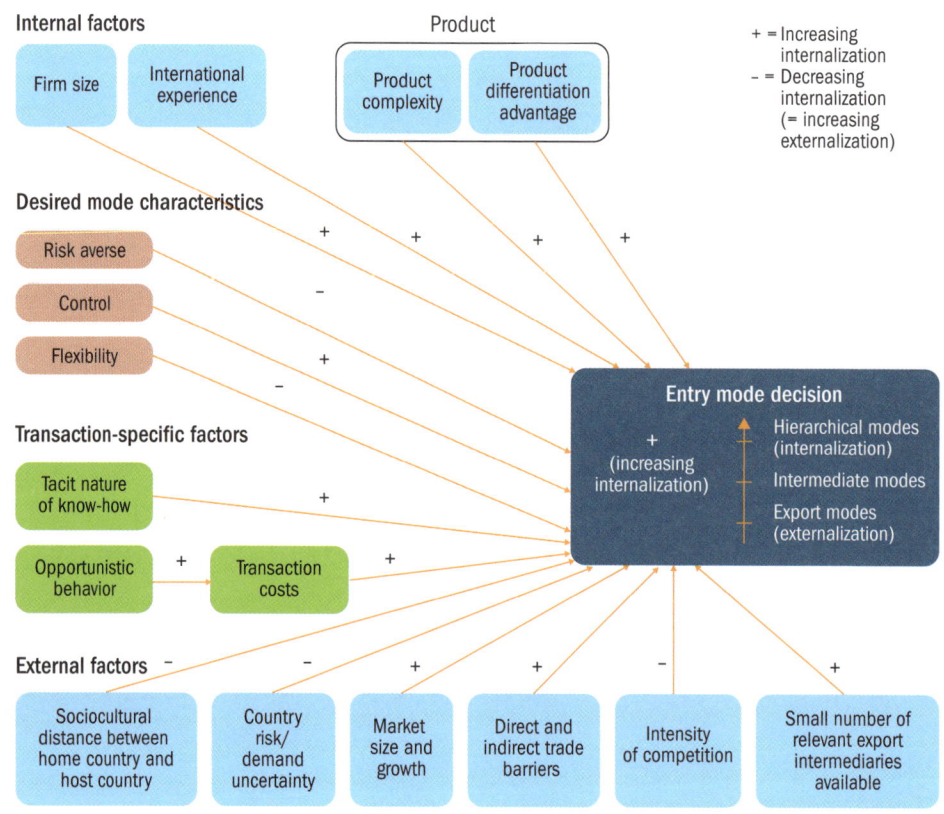

INTRODUCTION

When a company has decided which markets it is expanding to (see Hollensen's funnel model, page 200), it must choose what type of organization ("entry mode") shall handle the penetration of the company's products and services in the selected market. The model demonstrates the overall entry modes a company may choose from and what factors affect this decision and how.

WHAT IS THE MODEL ABOUT?

The model contains groups of variables that influence the choice of an entry mode in a specific market. Next to each specific variable, a plus or a minus sign indicates a recommended entry mode, evaluating whether this variable will increase or decrease the need for internalization. A "+" suggests moving towards "internalization," which originates from performing "internal" activities with a high degree of control. Operating its own subsidiary, the producer has a high degree of control of the activities in the specific market. A "-" will affect the choice of entry mode in the direction of relatively low control, i.e., primarily the choice of agents or importers/distributors.

GROUPS OF VARIABLES (FACTORS)	TYPICAL CHARACTERISTICS
Internal factors (including product)	A company's size, international experience, and product(s) are internal factors that influence the choice of entry mode in many ways. For example, the more complex the company's product, and the more the product differentiates itself from the competition, the further it points towards internalization. A high degree of control of activities in the local market is desirable, as it can be difficult to transfer highly complex knowledge or skills related to the product to an external partner, such as an agent, who might easily misunderstand certain aspects. In addition, a large company and a high degree of international experience will lead towards its own subsidiary. This is because the company already has experience with its own subsidiaries from other related markets.
Desired "entry mode" characteristics ("desired mode characteristics")	If a company wants to avoid risks, it is "risk averse," which points towards "export modes," i.e., choice of agent or importer solution. If a company desires a high degree of control, it must choose its own subsidiary company. If a company desires high flexibility, it must use "export modes" that can be replaced relatively quickly.

Transaction-specific factors	Transaction-specific factors are included in the transaction cost theory.
	For example, if there is a high degree of tacit know-how it will be difficult to include these factors in contracts and collaboration agreements.
	These are better exchanged within their own ranks, i.e., within its subsidiary company as, otherwise, there is a risk of opportunistic behavior by the agent.
	Opportunistic conduct (behavior that promotes one's self-interests) may occur from both the agent and manufacturer. This type of behavior promotes inertia and enhances trade transaction costs between the two parties, as the manufacturer, for example, must use resources to keep an eye on whether the local agent fulfills the contract and does not cheat in any way.
External factors	A great social and cultural distance to the market and/or a high country-specific risk will cause the company to go in the opposite direction of "internalization" (thus the minus indicated in the model) toward "export modes," thereby outsourcing country-specific risks to a local external partner (e.g., a local agent).
	A large, local market with high-growth will, all things considered, result in the use of a subsidiary company. The subsidiary's steep fixed costs will be financed through a reasonable market share in a large market with high growth.
	Direct and indirect trade barriers (e.g., direct duty on exports of agricultural products to the United States) suggest the company opens a production company in the market to avoid customs duties.
	In the event of fierce local competition, the solution might be to outsource the risk to an external partner, for example, a local agent.
	Finally, if there are only a small number of relevant export intermediaries (e.g., agents) present on the local market, it might be a good reason for choosing a separate subsidiary. The few agents present can take advantage of the situation by demanding a higher royalty from the manufacturer.
	This will cause increased transaction costs and indicate "internalization."

HOW CAN YOU USE THE MODEL?

The model can be used to evaluate the type of marketing organization or operation that should preferably be used, taking into account the company and local characteristics. The model also provides an overview of the internal and external factors relevant to this evaluation, and how they each play a role.

WHAT ARE THE SHORTCOMINGS AND WEAKNESSES OF THE MODEL?

The model is a so-called ideal type model. It adheres to a general process, featuring key relationships; it rarely unfolds exactly this way but usually follows the described pattern.

The model indicates the main factors affecting the choice of "entry mode." However, there could be other factors that influence this choice. These "other factors" may depend on the specific business characteristics, market, etc.

The individual variables influence on the choice of entry mode are based upon an everything-else-alike consideration, not taking into account the possible simultaneous impact of other variables. By combining individual variables, and trying to get them to work together, the arguments become more complex and non-transparent.

Some researchers (including the below-mentioned Koch, 2001) argue "Market Selection" (via the funnel model) also provides input into which "entry mode" to use, so only one decision-making process is necessary instead of two. Or perhaps the company already maintains the position it wishes, to control the local marketing efforts as much as possible, and therefore, has already chosen a subsidiary setup. However, despite objections, the company should consider the factors impacting the choice of entry mode, regardless of market choices already made.

REFERENCES

Hollensen, Svend (2017). *Global Marketing*, 7th edition. Harlow: Pearson Education Limited.

Koch, Adam J. (2001). Selecting overseas markets and entry modes: Two decision processes or one? *Marketing Intelligence & Planning*, 19 (1): 65-75.

Root, Franklin R. (1994). *Entry Strategies for International Markets*. Lexington: Lexington Books.

HOLLENSEN'S GLOCALIZATION MODEL
By Svend Hollensen

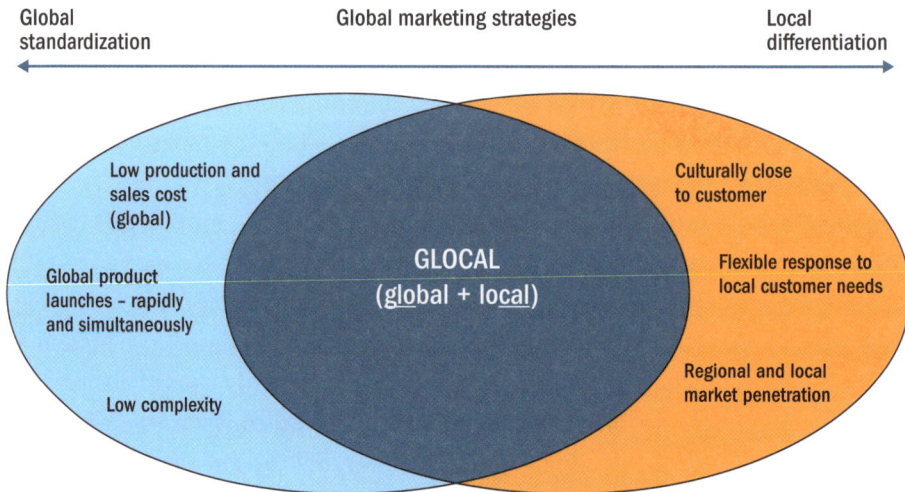

INTRODUCTION

The model demonstrates how a company, when entering international markets, can pursue a global strategy, local strategy or combination of the two: a glocal strategy. The model also shows the main advantages of the global and local strategies a company seeks to optimize simultaneously through the glocal strategy.

WHAT IS THE MODEL ABOUT?

By using the model, one can determine the factors, pushing or pulling a company towards globalization or localization. The company chooses where it wants to be on a scale from 100 % globalization (cross-border standardization) to 100 % localization (complete customization to the individual market, i.e., complete differentiation).

STRATEGY	EXPLANATORY FACTORS
Globalization	By standardizing across borders, the company achieves a low degree of complexity, including in production, thereby enabling the company to exploit economies of scale with lower unit costs.
	The company saves time by launching the same products and services worldwide. In today's competitive market, "speed" has become a crucial competitive parameter, especially in the IT industry. Examples of products that follow a clear globalized strategy include streaming audio (Spotify) and videos (Netflix), smartphone apps, and certain global brands such as Coca-Cola.
	Benefits of the strategy: Low unit costs, unambiguous global message.
	Disadvantages of the strategy: Lack of local adaptation of the strategy causes local customers to feel their needs are not being addressed.
Localization	By being local, the company is culturally closer to its customer. This enables the product to be better adapted to the needs of the customers, which also allows for more timely coordination of product launches in different parts of the world.
	Benefits of Strategy: Happier customers – they feel their locally determined needs have been respected.
	Disadvantages of the strategy: Very expensive to customize and design a marketing mix for each local market.

Glocalization	In the case of glocalization, upstream features (i.e., product development and production) are typically globalized and standardized, while adjusting the downstream (marketing and market communication) features to the local market. Both globalization and localization benefits are utilized at the same time. Production often takes place through modularization, which means basic modules of the product are mass produced, and eventually special features adapted to local markets will be added in the last part of the production process. This modularized production method is often used in the car industry. This method also applies to packaging, where packaging shape is adapted locally, although the content, such as detergent, is the same. *Advantages of the strategy*: Economies of scale in production while, simultaneously, achieving happier customers, as they feel that their local needs are met. *Disadvantages of the strategy*: Can be expensive and difficult to coordinate which value chain functions should be globalized (standardized) and which should be localized (differentiated across borders).

HOW CAN YOU USE THE MODEL?

The model can be used to exploit advantages from both a global and a local strategy. The model also provides an overview of the most important advantages using global or local strategies.

WHAT ARE THE SHORTCOMINGS AND WEAKNESSES OF THE MODEL?

The model is referred to as an ideal type model, which indicates that the "glocalization" is the perfect combination. However, the degree of glocalization can vary greatly from product to product and from business to business. Every company must decide its position and its various value chain functions. Of course, the company may also have different placements on the scale if it has different SBUs, which require the use of different degrees of globalization and localization.

REFERENCES

Andersen, Ole E., Poul K. Faarup & Svend Hollensen (2019). *Moderne markedsføring*, 3rd edition. Copenhagen: Hans Reitzels Forlag.

Hollensen, Svend (2017). *Global Marketing*, 7th edition. Harlow: Pearson Education Limited.

Hollensen, Svend & Christian Schimmelpfennig (2015). Developing a glocalization strategy: Experiences from Henkel's product launches in Middle East and Europe. *Journal of Brand Strategy*, 4 (3): 201-211.

Svensson, Göran (2001). "Glocalization" of business activities: A "glocal strategy" approach. *Management Decision*, 39 (1): 6-18.

DIGITAL MARKETING MIX
By Kim Skjoldborg

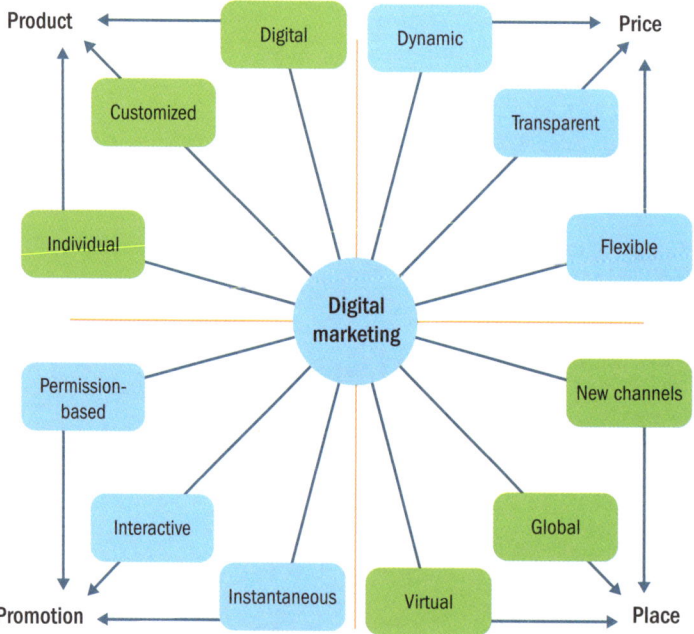

Reshaping the marketing mix

INTRODUCTION

The digital marketing mix is a further continuation of the traditional 4 P model invented by Jerome McCarthy in 1960. This model describes and visualizes the areas where digital marketing differs from traditional marketing.

WHAT IS THE MODEL ABOUT?

The model is about the company's parametric mix and the changes caused by digital marketing today being an integral part of corporate marketing. The shift towards more digital marketing changes the way in which parameters work. The model gives an overview of the most important changes that a company should be aware of.

Product: The product itself is often digital (for example, a movie) and that has some consequences. The advantage is that it is far less expensive to publish and that the distribution costs are lower. Digitalization also means that it is easier to customize and individualize products. An example is that customers themselves can customize the way in which their car, shoes or T-shirt should appear. This phenomenon is known by the term *mass customization*.

Price: Digitalization also has an impact on the company's pricing. The biggest difference compared to traditional marketing is that the price is far more transparent, i.e., customers have the opportunity to compare prices across different providers in a matter of seconds. This reduces the possibilities of price differentials. Over time, the difference between the online price and the price in the physical store has decreased. Transparency also means increased competition, and thereby, increased pricing pressure.

In addition to transparency, the price is flexible and dynamic, which means that it can be changed with short notice in both an upward and downward direction as demands fluctuate. For example, the price of a flight from Copenhagen to Paris varies according to the day of the week and the demand for that departure.

Digitalization has also meant the introduction of other price models, for example, auctions. A company can offer its product via platforms like eBay and sell it to the highest bidder.

Promotion: Market communication is significantly different from traditional marketing. An important difference is increased demand for customer's acceptance before contacting the customer directly, especially via email.

The terms *interactive* and *instantaneous* cover the recipient's ability to respond to the communication immediately. A reaction could be to visit the company's website, ask additional questions, share links or content or purchase the product. The time between exposure and response can be very short.

A quick response implies both risks and opportunities. Unhappy customers have the opportunity to comment on the company's activities, share content via social media and, in the worst case, trigger a shitstorm. Conversely, particularly satisfied users can recommend to others, become the best ambassadors of the company and directly instigate purchases from new customers.

Place: Place is a misleading word for distribution of a product or service. The crucial difference is that the company has added a new distribution channel. Especially in the entertainment industry – movies, music, and games – the product can be distributed directly from producer to the end customer. That way, the power of the distribution channel has shifted from the retailer back towards the producer. The owner of the product/service has gained more power, as the distribution can be carried out cheaper and faster digitally.

Digitization means a company is technically global the moment it creates a website. From that moment on, the company is visible to anyone who has access to the internet. A process that previously could take decades and cost considerable resources can be carried out in a relatively short period. Vice versa, as a consequence competition, is intensified within many industries as the number of potential competitors increases.

HOW CAN YOU USE THE MODEL?

The model can be used to obtain an overview of the consequences digital marketing has for the company's parameter mix. What separates the digital marketing mix from the traditional 4 Ps? Above all, the model can be used to develop and adjust the company's digital strategy.

WHAT ARE THE SHORTCOMINGS AND WEAKNESSES OF THE MODEL?

In general, the model has the same weaknesses as the traditional 4 Ps.

That is, the model lacks the last four or five Ps process: Physical Evidence, People, Policy, and Partnership (see 8 P model, page 56). Some believe that Partnership should be included, in particular, due to increased opportunities for relationship building that digital marketing holds.

A minor weakness of the model is that the individual parameters are difficult to distinguish. This is especially true for promotion and distribution. For example, digital products like movies and music can be marketed and distributed throughout the same channels. This means that the separation becomes more diffuse compared to the traditional model.

One final criticism is that the model views marketing from the company's perspective rather than the customer's, which is a weakness in relation to the Marketing Concepts' basic idea based upon the customer.

REFERENCES

Jobber, David & Fiona Ellis-Chadwick (2016). *Principles and Practice of Marketing*, 8th edition. Maidenhead: McGraw-Hill Education.

Chaffey, David & Fiona Ellis-Chadwick (2016). *Digital Marketing. Strategy, Implementation and Practice*. 6th edition. Harlow: Pearson Education Limited.

SOCIAL MEDIA LANDSCAPE
By David Juul Ledstrup

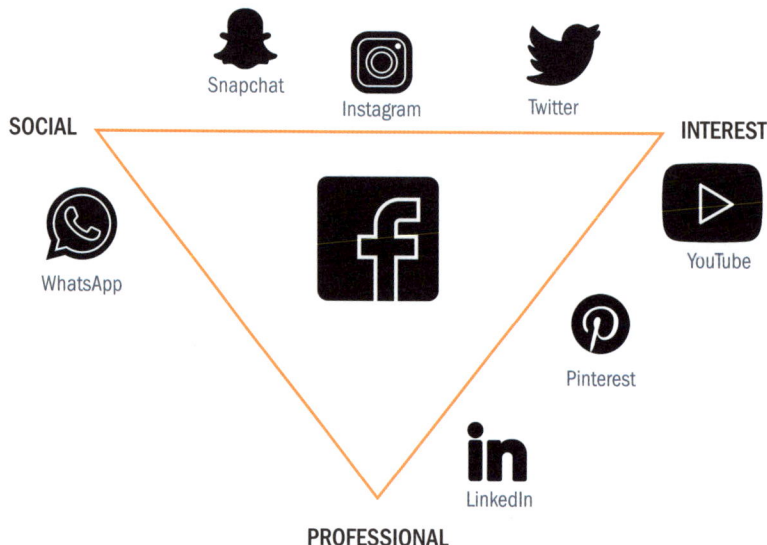

INTRODUCTION

The model describes the relationship between social media platforms and social media users, and their usage patterns – and thereby their motives to interact with each other on different platforms. The model, therefore, functions as a type of map whereby various social media can be placed to demonstrate their similarities and differences.

WHAT IS THE MODEL ABOUT?

When people are active on social media, they behave based on their relationship with other users. The model sets up three poles, where engagement is defined by personal-, professional-, or interest-based relationships. The model can map any type of social media, based upon the engagement patterns on each platform.

When social relationships are based on personal relationships with other users, the connection to another user requires a sense of personal attachment. Typical connections will include old and new friends as well as family members and personal relationships that develop in connection with recreational activities, workplaces, etc. Social relations go both ways, and the quality of the connection depends upon whether both parties choose to follow or befriend each other.

If the interaction derives from interest-based relationships, the connection to other users requires an association based on common interest areas, such as product interests, sports teams, political convictions, etc. Interest-based relationships can both consist of both parties following each other, and of one-way relationships where one user follows another user.

Professional relationships are created on the basis of users' professional networks and professional interests. Relationships typically occur as a result of users' current or previous workplace or their field of business, but may also occur as one-way relationships, like interest-based relationships.

HOW CAN YOU USE THE MODEL?

When assessing how to activate a target group, it is important to understand both the media platform – and why are users gathered there – and the behavior of users on the platform. The methods and users' perceptions of the message should be closely linked to whether a target group is being addressed in their personal sphere, interest sphere or professional sphere.

The model can be used to map out the current landscape for social media and assist when strategically assessing where and how to be present as the distributor of communication and content. The model also illustrates the type of relationships the individual platforms capitalize on when they want to target messages on behalf of other companies, for example, through advertising. Finally, the model illustrates how companies can position social media activities to attempt to compete and/or differentiate from one another.

WHAT ARE THE SHORTCOMINGS AND WEAKNESSES OF THE MODEL?

The model can be criticized for having a simplified view of user behavior. Although most social media platforms are traditionally "born" in one of the three poles, it is clear that some of the platforms are utilized by users to cultivate more than just one of the three types of relationships with other users. The model does not take into account changeable user behavior or platform development, whereby new features are constantly added, features that, in turn, affect user behavior.

REFERENCES

Bigum, Thomas (2017). Kursusmateriale. Copenhagen: Bigum & Co.

Facebook for Developers. The Graph API. Facebook for Developers. https://developers.facebook.com/docs/graph-api (retrieved 01.03.17).

Fitzpatrick, Brad & David Recordon (2017). *Thoughts on the Social Graph*. Bradfitz.com. http://bradfitz.com/social-graph-problem/ (retrieved 01.03.17).

Clampitt, Phillip G. (2018). *Social Media Strategy – Tools for Professionals and Organizations*. Los Angeles: Sage Publications.

MIT (2011). How the Interest Graph will shape the future of the web. *Entrepreneurship Review*. https://miter.mit.edu/articlehow-interest-graph-will-shape-future-web/ (retrieved 01.03.17).

COMPREHENSIVE SOCIAL MEDIA STRATEGY
By David Juul Ledstrup

	PROACTIVE	REACTIVE
HOME MEDIA	Publish	Manage
AWAY MEDIA	Activate	Monitor

INTRODUCTION

Social media strategies are often based solely on activities and usage of the individual media platforms. This model is used to elaborate strategies for all relevant social media across all social media platforms, as well as individual medias.

WHAT IS THE MODEL ABOUT?

The model provides a framework for developing strategies across the company's social media and the target audience's social channels. It also helps the company to structure its strategy both proactively and reactively.

Home channels include traditional "owned" and "paid" marketing channels on social media, platforms where you as a company control communications. It could be your own social media, such as a Facebook page or a Twitter account, but it could also be the company's website, newsletter or similar platform. *Away* channels are typical "earned" and "shared" media, e.g. your audience's Facebook profiles, websites or other channels, where the company does not have 100 % control of the communication. Both Home and Away, you can either be *proactive* or *reactive*. As a result, companies can create strategies in each area, all while focusing on the overall tactical direction. Regarding paid-owned-earned media (see the POE model, page 112).

HOW CAN YOU USE THE MODEL?

The model is used not only to create strategies across the company's presence on social media, but also to define tactical directions of each media. Each area of the model has an overall theme that defines the next steps in a strategy process.

Being proactive on your Home media, is primarily about what to publish as a brand or business. It opens up a number of comprehensive considerations, such as "On which media can our target group be best activated, and on what media do we therefore want to be active?" Then you can create strategies on the individual media. For example, if you want to be active on Facebook, it opens up a series of strategic considerations about the target audience, objectives of presence on chosen media, internal organization, and roles, content, etc.

If you have decided to be active on one or more social media platforms, you should now define strategies as to how you want to be reactive on your Home media, that is, how to manage inbound communication. Now we must start asking questions like "Who is responsible for answering inquiries?" and "How do we respond and in what tone of voice?" or "How do we measure whether our efforts are good enough when we respond?". These questions, coupled with other questions, help to define the strategy in the management phase.

A large part of social media success stories are often written when companies and brands are not necessarily pushing their messages to the target audience, but when the target audience is activated to speak positively about the brand or to share its message. A Proactive, Away strategy. This is accomplished by considering what a brand can do to get mentioned. Strategies must, therefore, be established, so consumers proactively make mention of the brand on social media.

Last but not least, strategies should be in place for what a brand decides to do when mentioned by others on social media. Reactive on Away media. That means the internet generally, and social media particularly should be monitored for conversations about one's brand or business, so you can respond to other people's channels. Both positive and negative responses should be foreseen and handled, for example, how to acknowledge praise or respond to a negative review before a shit storm occurs, at worst.

WHAT ARE THE SHORTCOMINGS AND WEAKNESSES OF THE MODEL?

Alone, the model cannot be used to precipitate precise strategies on social media. It can, therefore, be criticized for solely addressing what it takes to develop strategies, while not embracing the combined elements of an overall strategy.

REFERENCES

Andersen, Finn Rolighed, Bjarne Warming Jensen, Mette Risgaard Olsen et al. (2015). *International markedsføring*, 5th edition. Copenhagen: Trojka.

Andersen, Ole E., Svend Hollensen, Poul K. Faarup et al. (2016). *Moderne markedsføring*, 2nd edition. Copenhagen: Hans Reitzels Forlag.

Bigum, Thomas (2017). Kursusmateriale. Copenhagen: Bigum & Co.

Clampitt, Phillip G. (2018). *Social Media Strategy – Tools for Professionals and Organizations*. Los Angeles: Sage Publications.

Eiberg, Kristian, Sine Nørholm Just, Simon M. Torp et al. (2014). *Markedskommunikation i praksis*. Frederiksberg: Samfundslitteratur.

Kingsnorth, Simon (2016). *Digital Marketing Strategy: An Integrated Approach to Online Marketing*. London: Kogan Page.

AUTHOR PROFILES

AUTHOR	PROFILE
Kim Buch-Madsen	Kim Buch-Madsen is a business analyst and MSc (Econ.) with years of experience in the consulting industry, international retail chain, and self-employment. Kim taught strategy, marketing, and innovation at the Copenhagen Business School (CBS), Technical University of Denmark (DTU), and Danish School of Media and Journalism, as well as in leadership training. He is an accredited external examiner and author and co-author of several articles and books. https://www.linkedin.com/in/kim-buch-madsen-ba-88a6b
Ole E. Andersen	Ole E. Andersen is an MSSc., external lecturer at the University of Copenhagen and Copenhagen Business School (CBS). He is the head of the department for several marketing subjects and an accredited external examiner in several bachelor's and master's programs. Ole has extensive experience in market analysis consulting, as CEO of Dansk Reklame Film and as principal of the Advertising School in Denmark. He is the director of the consultancy Markedsdialog (Market Dialogue) and author of several books on marketing, advertising, and media.
Birgitte Grandjean	Birgitte Grandjean is a seminar teacher and holds a BA in business language and international business communication. She is a full-time teacher at KEA Design (Copenhagen Business Academy) in marketing, branding, and communication. Birgitte has more than 20 years of experience as a teacher and developing educational material and programs.
Christian Grandjean	Christian Grandjean holds an MA from the University of Copenhagen. He is a guest teacher and accredited external examiner at business academies and universities. Christian has more than 20 years of practical experience in marketing and communication at agencies and in companies.
Heidi Hansen	Heidi Hansen is a lecturer at the University of Southern Denmark, where she studies and teaches communication and branding with a particular focus on management. Heidi is the author and co-author of several books, including *Branding: Theory, Models, Analysis*, and is a popular speaker.
Niels Kühl Hasager	Niels Kühl Hasager holds graduate diplomas in Business Administration (Marketing and Organization) and an MBA. He is a lecturer at Cphbusiness Academy and guest lecturer at the Copenhagen Business School (CBS), Technical University of Denmark (DTU), etc. Accredited external examiner for Diploma of Leadership. He has many years of experience in the financial sector, entertainment industry, and market analysis consulting.

Author Profiles

Svend Hollensen

Svend Hollensen holds a Ph.D. and is employed at the University of Southern Denmark, where he is researching and teaching global marketing and B2B marketing. He is an internationally recognized author of a wide range of articles and books, including *Global Marketing* and *Marketing Management*. Svend currently holds several board positions and was awarded the BHJ Foundation's Research Prize in 2017.

Sine Nørholm Just

Sine Nørholm Just holds a Ph.D. and is employed at Roskilde University where she studies strategic communication with a particular focus on how technological and social developments affect communication work. Sine is the author and co-author of a wide range of articles and books, most recently, *Strategizing Communication. Theory and Practice.*

Jan Kyhnau

Jan Kyhnau teaches international marketing and business model design at University College of Northern Denmark. Jan is an experienced business model and value proposition designer and affiliated with the Business Design Center at Aalborg University. He is also a member of Alex Osterwalder's pre-reader team behind the *Value Proposition Design* book and has written about business models and value creation.

David Juul Ledstrup

David Juul Ledstrup is Head of Social Media for IPG Mediabrands and the Nordic advertising agency MARVELOUS. He is a former teacher and external examiner at business academies and is often used as a reference in nationwide newspapers, television and radio programs.

Michael Sjørvad

Michael Sjørvad holds an MSc (IM.) from the Copenhagen Business School (CBS) and is a lecturer in marketing and sales. For the past 17 years, he has taught and developed courses in many different areas. In addition, he has worked in development and research projects for business development.

Kim Skjoldborg

Kim Skjoldborg holds an MSc (Econ.) and is employed at the Lillebælt Business Academy, where he teaches various marketing subjects and science theory. Kim also teaches at the University of Southern Denmark and has many years of experience in the advertising and media industry. Kim won an award for the book *Media Planning*.